# the story of the
# THIRTEEN COLONIES

An engrossing account of the formation and growth of the original thirteen colonies, up to the time they seceded from England and fought the War of Independence.

# the story of the
# THIRTEEN COLONIES

## by Clifford Lindsey Alderman

*illustrated by Leonard Everett Fisher*

*Landmark* BOOKS

Random House · New York

For Patricia Smutney

This title was originally catalogued by the Library of Congress as follows:

**U.S.—HISTORY—COLONIAL PERIOD**

973.2
A

Alderman, Clifford Lindsey
  The Story of the thirteen colonies; illus. by Leonard Everett Fisher.    Random House ©1966
  187p   illus  (Landmark books)
  CONTENTS: The First settlement. - Pilgrims and Puritans. - The Story of New Hampshire. - New Netherland and New York. - The Jerseys. - Th Connecticut colony. - Lord Baltimore's noble venture. - The Smallest of them all. - How Delaware began. - William Penn's holy experiment. - The First of the Carolinas. - Land of rice and indigo. - The Last of the colonies. - The Coming of the revolution.
  1 U.S.—History—Colonial period   I Title

973.2

Printed in U.S.A.                    Random House
                              School & Library Service

Trade Ed.: ISBN: 0- 394-80415-5        Lib. Ed.: ISBN: 0- 394-90415-X

# CONTENTS

# chapter 1

# The First Settlement

The great city of London was getting ready to cele-
brate Christmas when three ships, the *Susan Constant,*
*Godspeed* and *Discovery,* sailed down the Thames on
December 30, 1606. The vessels were bound for the
New World. The largest, the *Susan Constant,* was of
only 100 tons burden, while the smallest, the *Discov-*
*ery,* was a tiny 20-tonner.

Aboard the ships were more than 140 persons. Some,
listed as "gentlemen," had no intention of doing any
work when they reached the distant land of Virginia.
They were thinking mainly of the gold they were sure
could be picked up with no trouble.

Many of these gentlemen were the younger sons of
English nobles. Under English law a nobleman's oldest
son inherited his property. The others had to find
ways of supporting themselves.

The rest of the colonists were of humbler birth. Some had signed for the voyage to escape the terrible conditions under which the poor lived in England. Others had come along because the trip offered excitement and adventure. There was not a woman or child among them.

John Smith, who would later write an account of the voyage and the settlement of Virginia, was not listed as a "gentleman." But he was no ordinary person, either. A short, sturdy man of 27, he looked as if he had a ramrod down the back of his doublet. Like the men of quality, he wore knee breeches, boots with flared tops reaching halfway to his knees, shoes with bows, and a broad-brimmed hat. A beard and a long, thin, ferocious mustache that curled at the tips decorated his face.

Money for the venture had been provided by the London Company, which hoped to earn a handsome profit. First and foremost, the settlers were to find gold. They were also to seek a passage to the South Sea (the Pacific Ocean) which would be shorter than the long one around Africa. Such a passage would provide a speedier and safer route to the spices, silks and tea of the East Indies. A third objective was to find the colonists sent to America by Sir Walter Raleigh in 1587. Raleigh's colonists had landed at Roanoke Island. But four years later, when ships returned there,

the colony had vanished and nothing was known of its fate.

The voyagers' Christmas was not merry. They spent it in the English Channel, beset by adverse winds. Six weeks passed before the wind shifted at last.

John Smith's air of self-confidence, his vigorous personality and his common sense won him respect. Many of the colonists, however, could not stand his know-it-all ways. For a time he was surrounded by an open-mouthed audience when he told incredible tales of his adventures. But some of his listeners who had had no such thrilling experiences became jealous.

As a very young man, Smith had made his way to Hungary to fight the Turks who had invaded that country. According to the stories he told, he had slain the gigantic Turbashaw, their leader, in combat, and cut off his head. He had fought in bloody battles, and religious pilgrims had thrown him overboard from a ship as an unbeliever. He had been captured and sold into slavery in Turkey.

At least so said John Smith, and who was to deny the truth of it? But his enemies circulated a story that he planned to seize control of the colony in Virginia with the aid of some confederates. Worse yet, they claimed he intended to murder the leaders of the expedition and make himself king.

He was arrested for mutiny and clapped into irons.

When the fleet arrived in the West Indies, a gallows was constructed to hang him. Luckily, not only for him but for the rest of the colonists, cooler heads prevailed and he was not executed.

Early in May, 1607, the vessels entered Chesapeake Bay. At the mouth of a river which the colonists called the James, after King James I of England, they established a settlement. It was named Jamestown. The land was marshy, and therefore unhealthy, and the water was impure. But the site did have a good anchorage where the ships could tie up to trees. It could also be defended against Indian attacks.

The London Company had appointed seven settlers as a council to govern the Colony. One of the seven was John Smith. Although he was no longer confined, Smith was still charged with mutiny. So the others forbade him to sit on the council.

The colonists pitched tents they had brought with them. For a time they were too busy looking for gold to put up more substantial houses. Nor did they think of how they were to exist once their scanty supply of food ran out. During the summer the heat and humidity of the Virginia coast exhausted them. Great numbers fell ill from dysentery and malaria. Before the summer was over, half of them were dead.

They found no gold nor any trace of the lost Roanoke colonists. And at last they had to face the approach of winter and the problem of food.

Without John Smith they would have been lost. They had expected to trade hatchets, beads, copper and other goods with nearby Indians for food. But the natives refused to give up the precious corn and beans they had raised to get them through the winter. Smith, however, made voyages to other Indian villages on the bay and its tributary rivers. By shrewd bargaining he obtained enough food for the colony to survive until spring.

He showed the settlers how to build a fort of logs. They also put up crude houses, plastering the log walls together with clay, and thatching the roofs with rushes. And they enclosed the village with a palisade, or stake fence.

The leaders were now convinced that Smith was innocent. They dismissed the charge of mutiny and let him sit on the council.

On one of his exploring trips to an Indian village, Smith was brought before Powhatan, powerful ruler of a confederacy of tribes. The gray-headed, scowling chieftain ordered his braves to seize Smith and force him to the ground so that his head rested on two great stones. The warriors then prepared to beat him to death with clubs.

The story of how Powhatan's beautiful young daughter, Pocahontas, saved Smith's life is famous. She is supposed to have rushed in and thrown herself down with her head resting protectively on his. Some historians have claimed that this happened only in Smith's fertile imagination. Other reputable scholars believe that the account is true.

Because of Smith, the colonists survived the winter. And in the spring of 1608 a ship arrived with supplies and approximately 100 new settlers. That fall another vessel brought about 70 more. They included two women, and one of them soon married.

But the colony's difficulties were not over. During the summer a fire destroyed Jamestown. The disaster had one good result, however. When the settlers rebuilt the town, they put up better houses.

In the fall, John Smith was elected president of the council. This virtually made him the colony's governor. For the first time there were signs that the settlement might succeed. Some of the newcomers were skilled at making pitch, tar and glass, as well as soap. And Smith made another deal with Powhatan for a shipload of corn to carry the colony through its second winter.

Although Jamestown survived under Smith's guidance, his wise but erratic rule was doomed when the king ordered a new charter drawn up for Virginia. Under it the colony was to have a regular governor. Until one could be appointed, the king sent Sir Thomas Gates to rule temporarily as lieutenant governor.

Before Gates could arrive, fate took a hand in John Smith's future. While he was returning from a voyage up the James River, a spark accidentally ignited his powder bag. Instantly his clothes caught fire and he became a flaming torch. He jumped overboard, quenching the fire, but he was already terribly burned.

Reaching Jamestown more dead than alive, Smith decided to sail for England aboard a vessel which had arrived with more settlers. Thus ended John Smith's connection with the colony. But his energy, resourcefulness and determination had already done much to save the settlement.

During the winter that followed, famine all but wiped out the colony. When the last of the settlers' moldy, maggoty corn meal was gone, they devoured dogs, cats, mice, snakes and horses, including the hides. By spring, only about 65 were still alive.

Then two ships arrived, and with them came Sir Thomas Gates. The disheartened colonists demanded that he take them back to England. Early in June, 1610, the handful of survivors, who looked like so many skeletons, boarded the vessels and sailed down the James.

Suddenly they sighted ships entering the river. The new governor, Thomas, Lord De la Warr, was arriving with food, supplies and 150 new settlers. The departing vessels sailed back to Jamestown. Virginia was saved.

From then on the colony grew steadily. More colonists came. Young people among the settlers married and had children. The most famous of these marriages was that of a sturdy young colonist named John Rolfe to Powhatan's daughter, Pocahontas.

As its population increased, the Virginia colony spread out. The coastal plain along Chesapeake Bay was a pleasant and fertile land. Streams flowed gently through it, including four broad rivers—the James, Mattaponi, Rappahannock and Potomac. Ships could sail up them as far as the rapids or falls that marked the limit of the tides. Thus the region came to be known as the Tidewater. These rivers took the place of roads and connected the increasing number of settlements rising on their banks.

Now Virginia needed some means of income. The colonists could exist by raising corn, beans, livestock and other agricultural products, but they had no way of obtaining manufactured goods like cloth, tools, iron ware and building materials. They had been accustomed to having all these things in England.

John Rolfe, Pocahontas' husband, is alleged to have solved the problem. He had an inquiring mind, and he wondered why the tobacco he raised was so poor. The Indians had taught the settlers how to grow it, but it was harsh and bit the tongues of those who smoked it.

In England, the British imported tobacco from the Spanish-held islands of the West Indies. In 1612 Rolfe obtained some seeds of this much milder variety and planted them. His crop was far superior to the Indians' tobacco. Then, in 1614, he shipped some to England, where it sold promptly. Soon he found better ways to cure the tobacco, so that it was even milder. His neighbors began to raise the new kind, too. This was the beginning of Virginia's tobacco industry. It brought great prosperity to the colony and had a tremendous influence on its future.

The colonists shipped their tobacco to merchants abroad, who sold it for them and bought the things the Virginians needed. There was no longer a great need to establish manufacturing.

Soon almost everyone was raising tobacco. There were problems, however. After three crops had been grown on a piece of land, the soil was exhausted. The settlers then had to clear more land. As a result, the settled area of Virginia expanded very rapidly.

Plantations—the large farms needed to supply more and more tobacco—sprang up throughout the Tidewater. Pioneers began to penetrate westward beyond the falls or rapids which blocked further navigation. First they settled the foothills of the Blue Ridge Mountains, known as the Piedmont. Then they pushed into the area called the Valley, between the Blue Ridge and the main range of the Appalachians. The men built roads to bring tobacco to the falls.

Settlers who had heard of the money to be made from tobacco flooded into Virginia. Many who came from England were too poor to afford the cost of the voyage to America. Virginia planters would pay their passage. In return the newcomers signed contracts known as indentures, promising to work for the planter until the debt was paid. These indentured servants were largely hard-working, ambitious people. After they had paid their debt, they soon bought land for themselves. Some became wealthy and prominent in the colony's government.

Thus Virginia grew and prospered. Many planters lived in comparative ease and sometimes in luxury. They entertained lavishly in splendid houses on their extensive plantations. In return for news of the outside world, they would give travelers comfortable lodging and fine fare. "Virginia hospitality" became famous.

Tobacco was so easy to raise and so profitable that no one wanted to do anything else. Other agricultural products such as timber and furs were used mainly for the settlers' own needs. Tobacco was king. It could legally be used instead of money to pay taxes, wages and debts. But in some years so much tobacco was raised that its price went down. With it went the colony's prosperity, so that everyone suffered.

Historians believe that the first Negro slaves were brought to Virginia about the year 1619 and sold to tobacco planters. The plantation owners found that it was cheaper to buy a black man than to pay wages to a white man. A slave could be forced to serve all his life without pay, but a hired laborer might demand a higher wage or leave at any time for a better job. As slavery increased, it brought untold trouble to Virginia, as well as to other southern colonies.

There was little religious persecution in Virginia. Most of the early settlers were members of the Church of England. Under the colony's charter this was supposed to be the only religion, but settlers of other faiths were allowed to live in peace.

The greatest problem was the colony's government. Under the first charter, the settlers were given all the liberties of Englishmen except that they had no right to govern themselves. Actually, however, the government in England did not interfere with the way the council in Virginia handled affairs.

Then in 1619 each of the settlements was allowed to elect two representatives or burgesses to a legislature. This body, along with a governor appointed by the king, plus the governor's council, formed the General Assembly. The Assembly made the laws and enforced them, although its actions had to be approved by the king.

For a number of years the British rulers were too occupied by problems at home to concern themselves very much with their colonies in the New World. Then in 1660 Charles II came to the throne. To the dismay of the Virginians, the new king decided his colonies in America enjoyed altogether too much independence. Laws were passed in England, requiring that certain American products—among them tobacco —be exported only to England and only in English ships. Virginia planters had previously been using Dutch vessels, which charged lower freight rates. And much of the Virginians' tobacco was being sent to other European countries, where import duties and other charges were lower than in England.

The governor of Virginia at the time was Sir William Berkeley. Sir William went to England to ask that these restrictions under the new Navigation Acts be removed. He was both surprised and aggrieved to have his request curtly refused. Moreover, he was told to "repair speedily" to Virginia.

Up to that time Sir William had done good things for Virginia and earned the love of the people. But after he returned from England he grew more and more tyrannical. He maneuvered to get burgesses elected who would support him. By rewarding those who did his bidding and severely punishing those who did not, he kept his power.

For a good many years Virginia had had little trouble with the Indians. But the redmen were becoming more and more restless as they saw their lands and hunting grounds grow smaller each year.

In January of 1676 they struck, destroying 60 plantations and murdering 36 people in 17 days. Planters demanded that Berkeley send troops against them, but he refused. He feared that such an action would cause friendly tribes around Jamestown to attack. Then, in May, the Indians raided a plantation belonging to a young settler named Nathaniel Bacon, and killed his overseer.

The hot-headed Bacon gathered together a group of planters and drove the marauders into the western mountains. Then, having been elected a burgess, he came to Jamestown for the session of the General Assembly. At Jamestown Berkeley had him arrested as a rebel.

Bacon apologized to the governor and was allowed to take his seat in the Assembly. Then he heard he was about to be arrested again, so he fled from Jamestown. Berkeley ordered him seized. Bacon soon returned with a force of 520 angry planters. Berkeley called for troops to defend him, but few responded.

Bacon and his supporters, burly, uncompromising men in the buckskin dress of the frontier, marched to the statehouse door. Berkeley came out to meet Bacon.

They faced each other—the governor aristocratic in fine velvet, his face inflamed with outraged dignity; Bacon, tall, slender, black-haired and scowling.

"You, sir, are a traitor!" roared Berkeley. He drew his sword. "Let us settle this matter with a duel!"

"Sir," Bacon replied, "I come not nor intend to harm a hair of your Honor's head, and as for your sword, your Honor may please to put it up. It shall rust in its scabbard before I shall ever desire you to draw it. I come for a commission against the heathen who daily murder and spill our brethren's blood, and a commission I shall have before I go!"

Berkeley gave him the commission, but treacherously revoked it as soon as the rebels had left. Again the governor declared Bacon a traitor. When Bacon came after him once more, Berkeley fled to safety on the other side of Chesapeake Bay. There he called English warships to his aid, raised a force of 600 men and returned to Jamestown.

Bacon marched again for the capital. Most of Berkeley's force deserted, and the governor took refuge aboard one of the warships which had carried him across the bay. Bacon realized he could not defend Jamestown against the vessels' cannon, so he set the town afire and destroyed it. The future of the colony seemed uncertain.

But the young planter was worn out from the strain of leading the rebellion, and a few days later he fell ill of a fever and died. Bacon's Rebellion collapsed and Berkeley's government was restored. After that, on the whole, the Virginians and the royal governors got along fairly well.

Meanwhile, England was engaged in a long series of wars with France which lasted off and on for more than half a century. In America they were known as the colonial wars. The battles were fought largely between the French in Canada and English troops aided by men from the northern American colonies.

Virginia was far from Canada. For some time it took no active part in the struggle. Then the French reached Fort Du Quesne, where the Allegheny and Monongahela rivers meet to form the mighty Ohio. In this position they were a threat to the Virginians.

An English general, Edward Braddock, led his army westward, fell into an ambush of French and their Indian allies and was routed with terrible losses. But the Virginia militia who went with Braddock gained invaluable experience despite the defeat. Their training stood them in good stead later. Many of them became able officers in the American Revolution. As for the young Virginian who commanded them,

Colonel George Washington, he would lead America to victory in that war.

It is not easy to say which American colony had achieved the greatest prosperity by the middle years of the eighteenth century. Certainly Virginia was among the leaders. And if a gracious way of living made possible by prosperity is to be considered, the colony must stand in the topmost rank.

# chapter 2

# Pilgrims and Puritans

The colonists who set out from Plymouth, England, on September 6, 1620, in the *Mayflower* were quite different from the original settlers of Virginia. There were no "gentlemen" among the more than 100 passengers. None of them expected to make easy fortunes by picking up gold. All were determined to work hard and succeed in the New World in spite of the adversities they knew must lie ahead.

Less than half were Separatists, people who had broken away from the Church of England. These Separatists had fled from England to a refuge in Holland, where they could worship in their own faith. But they feared their children would become Dutch in speech, ways and thought.

The Separatists called the other members of the expedition "Strangers." Some of the Strangers were going on the voyage to escape poverty and hardship in England. Adventure and a new life attracted others. It was fortunate for the Separatists that the Strangers had come along, for among them were men who would be sorely needed if the colony were to survive. Although the Separatists were the true Pilgrims, all the settlers came to be known by that name.

The expedition had made two earlier starts, forced back each time by the *Mayflower's* leaky companion, the *Speedwell*. Now all the passengers were wedged uncomfortably into the 180-ton *Mayflower*, and she set out alone.

It was nearly the middle of November before the ship anchored off what is now Provincetown, where the great hook of Cape Cod curls up like the tip of a lion's tail. While still aboard their vessel, the men drew up an agreement called the Mayflower Compact. Under it, just and equal laws were to be made for the good of the colony, and all the settlers were to obey them. Although they described themselves as loyal subjects of King James I, nothing was said about getting his approval of these laws. The colonists would govern themselves. Ashore, the weather was bleak. The narrow neck of land turned out to be a sandy waste dotted with bogs and stagnant ponds. In a small boat a party of men began seeking a better place to settle.

They found it on the opposite side of Cape Cod Bay, at Plymouth. There the *Mayflower's* passengers finally landed on December 21, 1620.

They lost no time in building their houses, though they worked through day after day of cold, dreary rain. While they lived in temporary huts, they put up an assembly hall and homes that were more permanent. The settlement stood along a little stream they called the Town Brook.

One thing mystified the colonists. Part of this place they had chosen had plainly been used at some earlier time for growing corn. This seemed an unmistakable sign of Indians, and the Pilgrims were alarmed. As soon as possible they mounted their cannon on the hill which rose behind the village. Yet as the days went on they saw not a single savage.

That was fortunate, for if they had been attacked the battle might have gone hard with them. Of all the colonists only one—a Stranger—knew much about firearms, let alone fighting. The settlers were fortunate in having this man, Miles Standish.

One of Standish's enemies dubbed him "Captain Shrimpe" because he was short and squat. He tried to make up for his small size by a pugnacious air and blustering manner. Like John Smith, he was experienced in warfare so he served as the colonists' military commander. The red-headed Standish eased their fears of attack and led a number of exploring expeditions into the unknown wilderness and along the coast.

The cold, winter weather, however, was the most serious threat the settlers faced. Although they had had the wisdom to provide themselves with enough food to see them through to spring, nearly half of the colonists died. At one time Standish and William Brewster, a Pilgrim elder, were the only leaders able to be up and active.

Yet all through these dreadful weeks, those who were well enough worked tirelessly to help the ill. Never once was there any thought of giving up. When the *Mayflower* sailed back to England early in April, not one of the settlers went with her.

In March, as the winter neared its end, an Indian strode into the village. To the settlers' amazement he hailed them in English: "Welcome!" He was Samoset, an Indian from the coast of Maine, where he had learned a little English from the crews of vessels which had come there to fish.

He and a companion, Squanto, became the great friends and benefactors of the Pilgrims. Squanto had gone to England aboard a ship which had been exploring the coast. He had stayed abroad for ten years. Upon his return he found that his tribe, the Patuxets, who lived at Plymouth, had been wiped out by a plague. Thus the mystery of the cornfields was solved.

Through their two friends, the colonists met the great chief Massasoit of the Wampanoags, who claimed all the lands in that part of America. Massasoit too became their great friend, and the treaty of peace he made with them remained unbroken for fifty years.

As the weather grew warmer, the settlers planted their first crop of corn, barley and peas. Squanto, who had come to live with them as interpreter, showed them how to plant the corn in hills. He also taught them how to fertilize it with fish which swarmed in the Town Brook.

Things went well with the Pilgrims now. The crops flourished. They had settled in a land of plenty. The bay teemed with cod, huge lobsters and clams. The streams were alive with eels and mussels. An abundance of grapes, berries and plums grew wild near by. There was excellent hunting for deer, ducks, geese and gobbling wild turkeys. That fall the Pilgrims gave thanks to God, and then all feasted in America's first Thanksgiving.

Other ships arrived with more settlers. There were marriages and children were born. During this time no one interfered with Plymouth's self-government. The settlers enjoyed all the liberties of Englishmen. They also had the religious freedom they had sought, though it was a stern and narrow-minded form of worship. Their leaders seemed to forget how the Separatists had been persecuted, for in turn they frowned on all other religions.

Meanwhile, other settlements were being started along the coast of vast Massachusetts Bay. The most important was at Boston, settled by Puritans in 1630. About a hundred settlers came first in the ship *Arbella*.

The Puritans were English Protestants who wanted to "purify" churches of priestly vestments and elaborate ceremonies. They said that their ideas on church organization and government came from the teachings of the Bible and the practices of early Christians.

Their leaders were substantial men, some of them wealthy, and they carried a charter from King Charles I. It permitted them to set up their own government and to pass laws, provided the laws did not conflict with those of England. Among the settlers were men who had professions or trades, as well as a number of indentured servants.

During the first six months of 1630 some 15 ships loaded with Puritan colonists made their way across the Atlantic. Before the year was out, Boston had about a thousand inhabitants. From the first the town was destined to prosper. Its people were ambitious and hard-working. Most fortunate of all, the settlement had a splendid harbor.

The soil of Massachusetts Bay was not as fertile as

that of the Chesapeake. Tobacco would grow, but its quality was poor. Since it could never bring the easy fortunes of Virginia, the Puritans had to find other ways to prosperity.

They learned to make things they needed instead of buying them abroad. Flax grew well. From it they made thread on their spinning wheels and wove it into the stout cloth called homespun. With their axes they hewed timbers and clapboards for their houses. The land produced corn and other vegetables. With the few crude tools they had, they whittled and fashioned dozens of articles needed in their daily life.

One important thing they lacked was iron wares— nails and many other articles of metal. They found earth rich in iron at the bottom of ponds and bogs. At the settlement of Saugus the first iron works in America was established in 1644. Here men smelted the ore and forged the iron into useful products.

Gradually, too, the colony built up a trade with Europe by which the settlers could buy some manufactured goods. Timber grew in abundance in the forests. With it they built ships. Shipyards sprang up. In Boston and other coastal towns the screech of saws, the *rat-tat-tat* of mallets and the scraping of adzes was heard as fine, tall vessels took shape on the stocks or building ways. Ropes were needed to fit out these sailing ships. The colonists planted hemp, from which the ropes were spun.

Some vessels ranged as far as Newfoundland, returning loaded with fish. Larger ships carried salt fish,
lumber, barrel staves and furs, especially beaver skins,
to Europe. Fish and wood products went to the West
Indies in exchange for dyewoods, sugar, fruit and
other cargo. Virginia traded tobacco for the staves
used for the hogsheads in which it was shipped. Massachusetts Bay soon bred a race of hardy seafaring men.

The settlers did not forget the importance of education. Unlike Virginia, where the plantations were far
apart and most children were taught at home, Massachusetts lost no time in setting up schools. The first
was established in Boston in 1635. By 1642 all towns
in the colony were required to have them. And in
1636, Harvard College, the first in America, was
founded.

All would have been well but for the growing
hostility of the Indians. When the great and good
Massasoit died in 1661, he was succeeded by his older
son, who soon died. The second son, Philip, whom
the Indians called Metacomet, became chief. Philip
was a great leader, but a bitter and sullen Indian who
hated the white men.

His hatred grew as new settlements sprang up
farther and farther west until they reached the fertile
valley of the Connecticut River. Philip saw that in

time the Indians would be driven from the great wilderness in which they lived, hunted and fished.

Having persuaded other tribes to join in a powerful confederacy, Philip launched a bloody war in 1675 in an effort to drive the white men out. All through the territory of Plymouth and Massachusetts Bay the Indian warriors swooped down upon settlements, burning the houses and killing the people.

The two colonies struck back with an army commanded by Governor Josiah Winslow of Plymouth. The troops marched through a trackless swamp to the hidden stronghold of the Narragansetts, attacked and burned it, and almost wiped out the tribe.

Philip was still powerful, however. And Winslow, though a good military leader, did not know how to cope with Indian warfare.

At last the daring, fearless Captain Benjamin Church of Rhode Island organized a band of rangers. He and his men were all crack shots and skilled at fighting in Indian fashion. They hunted Philip down in another dense swamp and shot him dead. With that, the Indians' power collapsed and King Philip's War ended.

But serious trouble of another sort was in the making. When King Charles II and his successors began to assert power over the American colonies,

Massachusetts bitterly resented it.

Like Virginia, Massachusetts was indignant over the Navigation Acts passed by the English Parliament. The Acts, of course, required that colonial exports must be carried only in English ships. All imports had to be produced in England or else brought there first and then shipped to America in English vessels.

The Massachusetts colonists, like the Virginians, knew that these products could be shipped cheaper in Dutch ships. And in Holland the merchants charged lower commissions than those in England for selling American products and buying goods to be sent to the colonies in return.

For years, American shipowners and merchants simply ignored the Navigation Acts. Then, in 1676, Charles II sent one of his men, Edward Randolph, to Boston with orders to investigate conditions in the New England colonies.

Randolph was an arrogant, meddlesome man, who came to America looking for trouble. In all, he made eight voyages across the Atlantic, and he so vexed the settlers that they heartily wished him at the bottom of it.

On his first visit, Randolph was outraged to see ships from a number of European ports anchored in Boston harbor in defiance of the Navigation Acts. But Governor John Leverett, a courageous man, bluntly told the King's agent that under its charter Massachusetts had the sole right to make laws concerning trade or anything else.

But Charles II was no friend of Puritans, and at Randolph's recommendations, the King issued a decree revoking the colony's charter. By a stroke of the pen, all the people's rights as Englishmen simply vanished. Charles II was now their master and they must do his bidding.

Then, after Charles' death in 1685, his despotic brother, King James II, appointed Sir Edmund Andros governor of "the Dominion of New England." Andros and his Council, also appointed by the King, could make the laws, subject to the King's approval, regulate the colonies' trade and impose taxes.

Andros was a stern man who insisted on strict obedience. For more than half a century the people of New England had governed themselves and elected their governors and representatives in the General Court, or legislature, which made the laws. Now they felt a tyrant had been sent to rule them.

Andros soon did a number of things the people felt were oppressive. All of New England seethed in fury.

Then, early in April, 1689, news reached Boston that the tyrannical James II had been chased from his throne by his aroused subjects. The settlers, equally aroused against the despot James had set over them, decided to be rid of him too. In Boston on the morning of April 18, drums thundered and rolled; men grabbed their muskets and poured into the streets to join the colony's militia. The mob, aided by the soldiers, seized the detested Randolph and other supporters of the governor and threw them in jail.

Andros fled to a fort near the harbor and refused to comply with the rebels' demand to surrender. The irate colonists took the cannon on the ramparts and aimed them at the fort's walls. Then Andros gave up and was arrested. The commander of a British warship in the harbor changed his mind about bombarding the town when he saw the cannon of all Boston's shore batteries and those on other ships in the harbor trained on his vessel.

Andros was put back in the fort for safekeeping. He disguised himself in women's clothes and tried to escape. After he had passed two sentries safely, a third noticed a man's shoes peeping out from under the "lady's" skirts, and the governor was caught. Later he was sent to England with a demand that he be tried for his oppression, though nothing came of it.

Luckily for Massachusetts, James II no longer was king. William of Orange had come from Holland to rule with Mary, his Queen, next in the Stuart succession to the English Crown.

Trouble of still another kind came to Massachusetts Bay during the years before the charter was revoked. Among the new settlers were some who did not agree with the stern ways of the Puritan religion. They wanted freedom to worship as they pleased. One, Roger Williams, was banished from the colony and he started a new settlement in Rhode Island. Another disbeliever, Mrs. Ann Hutchinson, was also banished, and she too fled to Rhode Island.

Quakers were likewise banished, and suffered constant persecutions when they refused to go. Four were hanged. Thus a colony conceived for religious freedom proved it could be intolerant, too.

William and Mary granted a new charter in 1691, but it did not restore the colony's full freedom to govern itself. Under it, Massachusetts Bay became a royal province and included the Plymouth colony as well as what is now Maine. The province was to have a royal governor and lieutenant governor appointed by the King.

The General Court was restored, but it was to have two houses. One, the Assembly, would have representatives elected by the people. The other was the governor's Council. The governor could disapprove of any law passed by the General Court if it did not please him.

The first of the royal governors was Sir William

Phips, a swashbuckling sailor and adventurer, who had been born in dire poverty on the coast of Maine. Phips' success as a treasure hunter had made him a rich man, and James II had knighted him. Later, while he was back in England, William and Mary appointed him royal governor of Massachusetts.

Phips returned to Boston to find the colony engaged in a shameful witch hunt. In nearby Salem Village, some cruel and mischievous children had been denouncing people as witches. They claimed that these innocent men and women were torturing them. The accused persons were thrown into jail, then tried, and some were executed.

This "plague of witches" spread quickly through the province. When Phips arrived, the jails were filled with wretched people awaiting trial as witches, some because spiteful neighbors had denounced them.

Sir William has been criticized for not acting swiftly to end such an abomination, but his task was difficult. In those days almost everyone believed in witches. At last, however, Phips began to realize what a terrible wrong was being done. When he learned that a plot was afoot to denounce his own wife as a witch, he rampaged into the Boston jail like one of the West Indian hurricanes he knew so well. He ordered the doors thrown open to release all the accused witches, and by vigorous measures put an end to the frightful persecutions.

Later some of his enemies demanded his removal as governor. Phips went to England to defend himself against the charges and died suddenly while waiting for his trial to begin.

After that, as governor succeeded governor, nearly all of them were plunged into strife with the legislature over the people's rights. Most of them were good men, but they were sworn to do the King's bidding and enforce laws enacted by the British Parliament. The laws generally limited the colony's freedom. Several governors were recalled to England when complaints reached the King, but others hung on and fought for years.

Meanwhile, the colonial wars were in progress. These wars lasted more than half a century while England and France battled for the mastery of North America. Massachusetts was seriously threatened because it was so near Canada, or New France. In 1745, Governor William Shirley sent an army to besiege the French fortress at Louisbourg on Cape Breton Island off the tip of Nova Scotia. Almost no one believed these untrained farmers and fishermen could capture the supposedly impregnable stronghold, but they did.

In all the colonial wars, Massachusetts troops fought side by side with English soldiers. Like the Virginians, many would use the experience they had gained in these struggles when the colonies began their fight for independence against Britain.

The story of Massachusetts is one of a people who strove against handicaps and hardships and made their colony thrive in spite of these difficulties. It has a proud heritage, too, in its rugged spirit of independence. The great statesman Daniel Webster expressed the colony's achievements in this way: "I shall enter upon no encomiums upon Massachusetts; she needs none. There she is. Behold her and judge for yourselves."

# chapter 3

# *The Story of New Hampshire*

In the spring of 1623 the ship *Jonathan* arrived off the New England coast at a place about fifty miles north from where Boston was later settled. She carried only a handful of passengers, perhaps as few as ten. No one knows the exact number. There were no women or children among them.

The ship's passengers saw before them a broad harbor where a river widened to meet the sea. The tides ran swiftly there, swirling as they ebbed and flowed. A dense, green forest wall surrounded the sparkling blue water, while mewing white gulls coasted and dipped overhead.

The *Jonathan's* passengers, under the leadership of David Thompson, had not come to America to escape religious persecution. Nor for the time being at least were they thinking of a permanent settlement. They had come to make money for a group of men in England known as the Plymouth Council. The Council had sent them to the New World. There was no danger that these settlers would starve, for they were provided with adequate provisions. They had plenty of tools and equipment, too, to carry out their jobs.

They were to catch fish and evaporate sea water to obtain salt for preserving them. They were also to cut timber and new lumber. These products would be shipped to England and sold. If the venture made money, the settlement would continue. If not, it would surely be abandoned.

The men settled on a point of land along an inlet which branched off near the mouth of the harbor. They called it Pannaway, a name they probably borrowed from the Indians.

The Indians called the whole region Piscataqua, meaning "the place where three rivers make one." Two smaller streams converged there with the main river, which Thompson named the Piscataqua.

The men built huts covered with bark, turf or clay and then fell to their work of fishing and lumbering. Among them were carpenters who put up racks and stagings on which to dry the salted fish. As soon as they could, they built a larger house for themselves. This also served as a fort for protection against any possible Indian attack.

Soon two London fish merchants, Edward and William Hilton, came with another group of settlers. They were sent by Captain John Mason, one of the early English explorers of the New England coast. The Plymouth Council, of which he was a member, had granted him all the land in the Piscataqua region. He decided to call it New Hampshire, since he was from the county of Hampshire.

The Hilton brothers pushed on up the Piscataqua about eight miles. There, at a point where the Cocheco flows into the Piscataqua, they established a settlement which would one day be known as Dover.

Captain Mason sent eight skilled Danes to assist the settlers. They built a mill to saw timber and another to grind grain. They also made potash from wood ashes. In order that the settlement might increase and continue, the Captain also sent 22 women.

Then, in 1631, the Hiltons started a settlement approximately three miles above Pannaway. The meadows along the shore there were lush with wild strawberries, which gleamed like rubies in the tall grass. The colonists called the place Strawberry Bank. It proved to be a better location than Pannaway, which never amounted to much.

Dover and Strawberry Bank grew slowly, for in a way the settlers were owned by Mason and the Plymouth Council. Everything they needed was provided for them, including food, building materials, guns and ammunition, tools, even fine fat cattle from Denmark. The men were paid wages like any other workmen and owned no land of their own. Thus they were not building a future for themselves in the New World. Only the proprietors benefited from their labor, so the settlers had little reason to strive for improvement.

In 1635, however, the Plymouth Council was forced to give up its charter to Charles I. Since the King had little time to think of his American colonies, the New Hampshire settlers now had a chance to govern themselves. Both Dover and Strawberry Bank set up governments of their own.

Meanwhile, a minister named John Wheelwright was banished from the Bay Colony on account of his religious beliefs. He was a brother-in-law of Ann Hutchinson, who had earlier fled to Rhode Island. Wheelwright came to New Hampshire and founded Exeter in 1638. The next year a group of Massachusetts Puritans settled at a place they called Hampton. For a long time Strawberry Bank, Dover, Exeter and Hampton were the chief towns in New Hampshire.

These were troubled years for the colony. The Puritans and the dissenters did not get along. In Dover, where some of Mrs. Hutchinson's followers had gone, there was strife. When Massachusetts laid claim to all of New Hampshire under its original royal grant of lands, the four towns were too weak and disunited to stand against the larger colony's demands. In 1641 New Hampshire came under Massachusetts' rule. It remained so for nearly forty years, and did not make a great deal of progress during that time.

When Charles II sent Edward Randolph to investigate the New England colonies, New Hampshire did not like him any better than its neighbor colony. However, he proved to be New Hampshire's benefactor. In an act of spite, perhaps, against Massachusetts, he recommended to the King that the two colonies be separated. In 1679 New Hampshire became a royal province.

Once that was done, prosperity came slowly but surely to the colony. New settlements were established in the wilderness to the westward. By 1735 they had reached the Connecticut River, though as yet there were none near the rugged mountains that have given New Hampshire its name of the Granite State.

Fishing was a profitable business, and logging in the immense forests became an even greater source of income. The colonists needed lumber for fishing boats, as well as for larger vessels to carry the settlers' products to Europe and the West Indies. The tall, straight pines were in demand for masts. Shipyards sprang up in Portsmouth, which had lost its charming name of Strawberry Bank. The settlement bustled now with activity. Large and small vessels of all kinds slid off the stocks into the harbor.

Portsmouth had become New Hampshire's largest and most prosperous town. There were many merchants so well off they could afford to build splendid houses.

At Dover, bricks were made from the excellent clay available in the area. "Bog iron" was discovered near several settlements and sold at Saugus, Massachusetts, until New Hampshire men built an iron works at Newmarket. Then the Assembly forbade shipment of the ore outside the colony.

Some Scotch Presbyterians who had settled in northern Ireland and been persecuted there also emigrated to New Hampshire. They founded the settlement of Londonderry. These people were hard-working and thrifty. In their homes they spun the beautiful lace they had learned to make in Ireland, as well as fine linen cloth. This, too, became an important industry.

Then came the colonial wars, in which New Hampshire suffered severely. Indians from Canada, sometimes led by half-savage French woodsmen called *coureurs de bois,* struck without warning at the colony's frontier villages. They burned houses, murdered settlers and carried off others to Canada. Few of these prisoners were killed, since they could be held

for ransom or sold to Frenchmen who kept them as servants.

The colony struck back when a New Hampshire man, Robert Rogers, organized a band of rangers. The rangers were bold, fearless men, skilled in the ways of Indians. They were also deadly shots with a musket. They surprised the Indian village of St. Francis, where most of the raids originated, burned it and destroyed most of its inhabitants. The story of this expedition by Rogers' Rangers and the fearful hardships they suffered as they returned through the wilderness by a roundabout way is one of the most thrilling in our colonial history.

Like the other colonies, New Hampshire resented the rule of the royal governors. But while the colony was a part of Massachusetts, the governors remained far away in Boston. Therefore the New Hampshire people had little trouble with them. Then in 1741 Benning Wentworth became the first royal governor of New Hampshire. For 26 years Wentworth ruled like a king, though he had been born right in New Hampshire, at Portsmouth. An autocratic, handsome man, he liked to impress the people by riding, clad in crimson velvet, through the town in his magnificent coach.

Although Wentworth was already a rich merchant, he wanted to make much more money. He did so by

granting land in the vast wilderness of the Green
Mountains west of the Connecticut River. Settlers who
bought acreage paid fees which went into Wentworth's
pocket. Soon he was able to build an immense, ram-
bling mansion on the outskirts of Portsmouth. It can
still be seen there today.

Among the Governor's staff of servants was a young,
pretty girl named Martha Hilton. Although she was
only a poor chambermaid, Martha loved fine clothes
and luxury. One day a scold took her to task for wear-
ing a dress which did not befit her lowly station.

"Never mind how I look!" Martha snapped. "I shall
yet ride in my own chariot," and she did. Governor
Wentworth, who was then 60, married her.

Trouble eventually developed in the region where
Wentworth had sold land for settlement. Known
today as Vermont, the area was then called the New
Hampshire Grants. The colony of New York claimed
ownership of the land. It sent sheriffs and their officers
to evict the settlers.

Ethan Allen, a hulking mountain of a man with a
voice like the blast of a typhoon, organized a lawless
band called the Green Mountain Boys to drive the
"Yorkers" out. There were fights and whippings and
finally even bloodshed, when a sheriff's man fired on
some of the settlers and killed two of them.

The dispute was not settled until after the Revolution, at the time Vermont became a state. By then Ethan Allen had won far more fame as the man who led the Green Mountain Boys against the British stronghold of Ticonderoga and captured it.

No other American colony was quite like New Hampshire. It had no large industries or even a highly profitable agricultural product like tobacco to make it rich. Yet it prospered and grew in a modest way. As for its people, Daniel Webster, who was born in New Hampshire and loved it, paid them a special tribute when he compared them to the Old Man of the Mountain. That is the rock formation in New Hampshire's White Mountains which looks like a great stone face.

He said, "Men hang out their signs indicative of their respective trades; shoemakers hang out a gigantic shoe; jewelers a monster watch; and the dentist hangs out a gold tooth; but up in the mountains of New Hampshire, God Almighty has hung out a sign to show that there He makes men."

# chapter 4

# New Netherland and New York

A small, bright-eyed, hard-working animal with a coat of sleek, soft fur was really responsible for the beginning of New Netherland. In 1609, the Englishman Henry Hudson sailed far up the majestic river which is named after him aboard his cockleshell of a ship, the *Half Moon*. When he reported that the river valley had great possibilities for trade, especially in beaver skins, the Dutch merchants who had sent him pricked up their ears. Beaver skins were valuable. In Europe fine beaver hats were worn by all who could afford them.

After that, traders voyaged to the Hudson River now and then, but for some years there was no permanent settlement. Then in 1624 the Dutch West India Company sent the *New Netherland* to America. The ship carried 30 families, part of whom were Dutch and part French-speaking Walloons who had fled to Holland to avoid religious persecution.

Eighteen families traveled up the Hudson and landed at the place where Albany now stands. There they built shelters for themselves and a little fort. They called their settlement Fort Orange.

Two years later, ships carrying more Dutch and Walloon colonists arrived in America. They landed on the island the Indians called Manhattan, where the Hudson River widens to form a magnificent harbor as it flows into the sea. There they established the settlement of New Amsterdam.

Aboard one of the ships, the *Sea Mew,* was Peter Minuit. The Dutch West India Company had made him director-general, or governor, of the new colony of New Netherland.

Minuit was a stocky man with graying hair, coarse ways and a blunt tongue. He ruled sternly and was not greatly loved by his people. But he is famous as a shrewd trader who made what is probably the most profitable land purchase in all history. For 60 guilders (about $24) he bought Manhattan Island from the Indians. Today a single square inch of that land would cost many times that amount. Peter Minuit also managed to remain friendly with the Indians who brought their beaver skins to the settlement.

An evil known as the patroon system began at this

time. The Dutch West India Company had granted enormous tracts of land along the Hudson River to wealthy men. These patroons or proprietors rented the land to settlers and ruled them almost as if they were slaves.

The situation did not improve when another domineering Dutch governor arrived in New Netherland in 1647. As his ship drew near the tip of Manhattan Island, Governor Peter Stuyvesant spied the diamond-shaped fort that surrounded his new residence. The fort's stone walls were tumbling into ruin. Inside, stood the sturdy brick governor's house, barracks for the soldiers, a jail, storehouse and a church. The houses that clustered about the fort were poor and mean.

New Amsterdam looked even worse when Stuyvesant came ashore. It was springtime, and the narrow, crooked little streets were mudholes. Pigs, dogs and goats wandered in and out of the fort through gaping holes in the walls. The whole place had an air of idleness and neglect.

Stuyvesant was not one to stand for such squalor. He was a man of great vigor and drive. And the only existing portrait of him shows a face that might have been cast of iron—stern, proud, determined, without a trace of a smile.

A cannon ball had shot off his right leg during a

battle in the West Indies. In its place, Stuyvesant wore a wooden one covered with shiny silver. As a result, the people of New Amsterdam called him "Old Silver Leg." They were to call him even worse names before the end of his 17-year stint as governor. He had a terrible temper, quarreled constantly, and ruled strictly.

But the new governor got things done. He set to work at once to make New Amsterdam a better place. Describing the fort as "more a molehill than a fortress," he ordered it repaired at once. He then had a protecting wall built across the island at the northern end of the settlement. (Today Wall Street runs where the wall did.) He encouraged trade, and New Amsterdam flourished. Its population increased from about 400 in 1647 to 1,500 in 1664.

Stuyvesant set the people an example of pride in their town. By 1660 many fine houses had been built of brick from Holland or stone quarried near by. The gable ends of the houses faced the street and were notched like flights of steps. This gave them a quaint look. Behind the houses were neat gardens with vegetables and flowers, especially tulips. These reminded the settlers of Holland. In fact, in many ways New Amsterdam looked like a smaller copy of old Amsterdam.

Stuyvesant had no patience with laziness or disorder.

He would go stumping about, belaboring idlers or breaking up street brawls with lusty strokes of his cane. He had no patience, either, with those who tried to interfere with the way he ruled the colony. His lack of patience finally got him into trouble.

New Amsterdam, like its successor, the City of New York, was even then a "melting pot" of many nationalities—Dutch, Walloons, Englishmen, Italians, Danes, Poles, Germans, Portuguese and Swedes. There was never much religious persecution in the settlement, probably because the inhabitants were of a number of different faiths. Many of the settlers had escaped persecution in their own countries. Now, however, they did want the rights of free men. But when they demanded a voice in the government of the town, Stuyvesant arrogantly refused.

The people decided to send a delegation to Holland to demand their rights from the States-General, which was like Parliament in England. Stuyvesant strove to prevent it, and even put one of the leaders in jail. But reports of the trouble had reached Holland. A letter came, ordering Stuyvesant to return there and explain to the States-General.

In a towering rage he tore the letter to bits. The order was later withdrawn, but Stuyvesant was forced to yield a little. The States-General granted the colonists a charter allowing them to elect representatives to govern New Amsterdam. For a time the stubborn governor insisted on appointing these burgomasters, as they were called, but he finally gave in.

New Netherland was doomed, however. The fact that it had been settled by the Dutch made no difference to Charles II of England. He proclaimed that the land was his, and in 1664 he gave it to his brother, James.

One fine morning in August of that year, Peter Stuyvesant fairly exploded in fury when he saw four great English warships riding at anchor in the harbor. Soon a summons to surrender was delivered to him. He tore that up too, but the English had caught him unprepared to resist attack. The fort could not hold out long against a siege, for there was little food to feed its few soldiers.

Although the doughty old governor was determined not to surrender, the people of New Amsterdam refused to fight. Perhaps they had decided they would have more freedom under English rule. The burgomasters urged Stuyvesant to give up.

At last he surrendered New Netherland, and it became an English colony. The name was changed to New York. New Amsterdam became New York City, and Fort Orange became Albany, all in honor of the colony's new proprietor, James, Duke of York and Albany.

The Dutch and other settlers were promised all the rights enjoyed by English colonists in America. Almost all of them remained, even Peter Stuyvesant. He retired to his pretty little *bouwerij*—the Dutch word for farm—north of the wall. Today that part of New York City is called the Bowery.

Under the English royal governors who followed, the people had more freedom. They elected representatives to an Assembly which made the laws. When Charles II died and James II became king, he abolished the Assembly. But after James was banished from the throne, the people demanded and were given a new legislative assembly.

The people also resented the great manors that had replaced the patroon system. These were large tracts of land granted to men who became very rich and powerful. The landowners held their farmer tenants under strict control and refused them some of the rights of free men.

As the colony grew and spread westward, land speculators bought vast tracts from the Indians and often cheated them outrageously. They then demanded high prices from settlers who wanted to buy farms. The speculators were protected in this practice by a succession of greedy governors.

The worst of these governors was William Cosby.

Haughty and arrogant, Cosby had a violent temper. He shamelessly took bribes from speculators, and engaged in land speculation himself. His corrupt ways led to a trial which is still famous today.

A chief justice of the New York Supreme Court, Lewis Morris, had a dispute with Cosby, and the governor removed him from office. Morris had been a fair-minded judge but the two men who remained both came from great land-owning families. They were merely tools of the Governor.

Morris and some other friends of freedom decided to start a newspaper, the *New York Weekly Journal,* to fight against the governor and his evil ways. They had little money, but they found a German printer, Peter Zenger, who would print the paper cheaply. It was filled with articles about a newspaper's right to print the truth and the right of a tyrant's subjects to resist him. The journal also championed the right of accused persons to a trial by jury, which Governor Cosby had refused to one of his enemies. Soon many people were reading the paper.

When articles criticizing Cosby kept on appearing, he swore to have revenge. It was well known that they were written by Morris and his other friends, but since they were not signed the governor could do nothing against the writers. Instead, he had Peter Zenger arrested for the crime of libel—publishing material which brings public shame or contempt upon a person.

Zenger, a poor man, was helpless and bewildered. Without powerful aid he would have had no chance against the vindictive governor and his friends, the justices of the Supreme Court.

But Morris and one of his friends, James Alexander, were both lawyers. They announced they would defend Zenger. Cosby then struck back by using his power to have them both disbarred from the practice of law.

Who would defend the poor printer? Morris and Alexander thought of the perfect solution, but they kept it a secret until the very day of the trial. On August 4, 1735, Andrew Hamilton of Philadelphia appeared in the crowded courtroom as Zenger's counsel. A gasp of dismay went up from the Governor's supporters, for Hamilton was considered the greatest attorney in America.

Chief Justice De Lancey had had far less experience than Hamilton. He made a mistake when he suggested that, while the jury could find that Zenger had published the articles, it might leave to the learned justices the question of whether the writings were libelous. The justices would know so much more about such matters than the jury, he explained.

At this Hamilton leaped to his feet. He told the jurymen that it was their right and their duty to decide the question of libel even though the justices were more learned. Then he defended his client so brilliantly that the jury brought in a verdict of not guilty.

The decision did much to establish one of the four great freedoms we know today—the freedom of speech and expression, which includes the freedom of the press. And thus the spirit of liberty stirred among the people of New York.

Meanwhile, as new immigrants flooded in from Europe, many settled on farms in the western wilderness of the Mohawk and Cherry valleys. Farming was profitable. Eighty percent of the people made their living by it.

In New York City, merchants became wealthy by dealing in furs, forest products, grain and flour. They shipped them abroad and in return imported manufactured goods the settlers needed. Like the neighboring New England colonies, New York traded with Europe and the West Indies. While it never became the seafaring colony that Massachusetts was, New York merchants needed ships, and shipyards were established to build them.

Again like New England, New York was seriously threatened during the colonial wars. There were few roads through the wilderness, but there was a water highway almost all the way from Canada. The enemy could strike by way of the St. Lawrence and Richelieu rivers, Lake Champlain and the Hudson. The French had their eye on Albany especially, since it was an important post for the fur trade with the Indians.

Soldiers from New York saw little action in the earlier wars, though there were Indian raids on the colony's northern outposts by savages from Canada. Luckily, the fierce Iroquois or Six Nations in the colony's western regions were allies of the settlers.

In the French and Indian War there was a great deal of fighting around Lakes George and Champlain, and New York troops were in the thick of it. Like the soldiers from other colonies, they profited by their experience. It prepared them well for the American Revolution.

As time went on, New York continued to flourish. It was most fortunate because of its resources. Blessed with a magnificent harbor at the mouth of the Hudson, it became a great trading colony. It had forest lands for producing timber products. In its river valleys the soil was rich.

While New York was being settled and enlarged, the fur trade provided a rich source of income. And the colony contained people of many nationalities, who were skilled in a variety of occupations. Because of all these advantages, New York achieved great prosperity and in time became known as the Empire State.

# chapter 5

# *The Jerseys*

For years New Jersey was actually two widely separated colonies. One, known as East New Jersey, was located across the Hudson River from New Amsterdam. The other, called West New Jersey, was far to the south along another broad, beautiful river—the Delaware.

When some of the Dutch in New Amsterdam crossed the Hudson in their boats, they liked what they saw. The land was heavily forested. The great trees, especially the tall oaks with their tough, hard wood, could be used in many ways. There was an abundance of wild fruit and nuts.

The Indians of the Lenni-Lenape or Delaware tribe who lived there grew fine crops of corn, beans and pumpkins. Game of all kinds roamed the woods. The waters of the river and harbor teemed with fish, oysters, crabs and lobsters. The shells of the oysters could be crushed and used to make mortar.

Yet for a number of years after New Amsterdam was founded, no one ventured to settle permanently in this region across the river. (The Indians called the area Hobocan.) Then in 1630 a member of the Dutch West India Company, Michael Pauw, was granted a large patroonship there. He was supposed to send settlers from Holland, but he did little about it. A few people, however, did cross from New Amsterdam. They built houses, and their settlement was named Pavonia after Pauw.

In 1643, and again in 1655, bloody wars broke out with the tribes in the region. Each time the Indians struck at defenseless little Pavonia and destroyed it. Yet each time the people of Pavonia, as well as those in other small settlements which had sprung up near by, eventually rebuilt their homes.

Gradually a few more colonists came to the west shore of the river and cleared land for farms. But Peter Stuyvesant had made New Amsterdam such a thriving town that not many people wanted to leave. And because Michael Pauw had sent no settlers, his patroonship was taken away from him. In 1664, when the English seized New Netherland, there were only about 200 colonists on the west shore of the Hudson.

During these early years, colonization was also beginning along the Delaware River. It was pleasant, rolling country, well suited for farming, and the river was like a highway over which produce could be shipped to market.

Swedish and Finnish colonists had settled on the west shore of the Delaware in what is now the state of Delaware. Soon they spread out, crossed the river and made a small settlement on the east bank. But old Peg Leg Stuyvesant considered this land to be part of New Netherland. He wanted no settlers there unless they were Dutch. In 1655 he led 600 soldiers in seven ships up the Delaware. The Swedes could do nothing against such might and they surrendered.

Then in 1664, the same year that the English took New Netherland, the Duke of York granted all of what is now New Jersey to Sir George Carteret and Lord John Berkeley. Berkeley became proprietor of the southern part, or West New Jersey.

All sorts of people now came to settle in the Jerseys, as the two colonies were often called. From New Netherland many Dutch settlers migrated to the valleys of the Hackensack and Raritan rivers in East New Jersey. Puritans who had come from New England to Jamaica on Long Island moved again to the area between the Raritan and the Passaic. Baptists from Rhode Island and Quakers from Long Island settled the shore from Sandy Hook to Raritan Bay.

More New Englanders came. Puritans from the New Haven colony in Connecticut migrated to East New Jersey and founded Newark, which today is New Jersey's largest city. These Puritans were narrow-minded people who wanted no inhabitants of other religions.

But Carteret and Berkeley drew up a constitution which gave the people great freedom in governing themselves. There was to be complete religious freedom, too. This attracted settlers of a number of different faiths to New Jersey.

Some of the people were still not satisfied. Instead of owning land they had to pay a small sum called a quitrent each year for the land they occupied. Most of the people now refused to pay these quitrents.

Sir George Carteret had sent his cousin, Philip Carteret, to be governor of East New Jersey. In 1672 the rebellious settlers organized their own Assembly and removed him from the governorship. The dispute was finally settled and Carteret returned as governor. But in 1680 the arrogant Sir Edmund Andros was made governor of New York. He claimed that all of East New Jersey belonged to New York.

Carteret was ready to fight, but before he could raise a force to resist, Andros sent soldiers to East New Jersey. They seized Carteret and he was put on trial in New York for governing without authority. The jury did not agree with Andros, and Carteret was acquitted.

Trouble with a more powerful tyrant soon came. When James, Duke of York, became King, he threatened the proprietors until they gave up the Jerseys to him. James II then made the two colonies part of a vast Dominion of New England, which also included New York. They remained so even for some years after James was ousted from his throne. Then they were returned to the proprietors.

During these years, West New Jersey was steadily growing. In 1675 a shipload of English colonists founded Salem, a short distance above the point where the Delaware River widens into Delaware Bay. It was the first settlement in New Jersey established by people arriving directly from England.

In 1677 the first Quaker settlers arrived. Pennsylvania is generally referred to as the Quaker colony, but the first Quaker settlement was actually in West New Jersey. The most famous of all Quakers, William Penn, was looking for a haven for the persecuted people of his faith in England. He and other prominent Quakers bought the rights to West New Jersey. The first arrivals founded Burlington, a little above where Philadelphia now stands on the opposite side of the Delaware. Some of the settlers were farmers, but more were tradesmen and craftsmen of the middle class. Others came as indentured servants.

Affairs went smoothly in the Jerseys for a time. Then in 1702 the two colonies were united into the single royal province of New Jersey. To prevent any jealousy between them, the combined Assembly was to meet half the time in East New Jersey's capital, Perth Amboy. The rest of the time they would convene in Burlington, capital of West New Jersey.

Unfortunately from 1702 until 1738, the governors of New York were also the governors of New Jersey. Since New York had a much larger population and was more developed, they spent most of their time there. New Jersey became a neglected orphan, and the people resented it.

Several of the governors were also unprincipled rogues. In carrying out the King's orders, a governor had great power. If the Assembly did not cooperate, he could dismiss it and order a new one elected. He could disapprove any law it passed. He appointed most of the colonial officials.

On the other hand, as in other colonies, the New Jersey Assembly controlled the spending of money and the levying of taxes. It could refuse to pay the salaries of the governor and his officials when there were disputes. In 1738 New Jersey was allowed to have its own governor, but the quarrels continued.

During this time the colonial wars were being

fought. New Jersey, however, was in no great danger, so it paid little attention to the earlier struggles. Nor was it happy when asked to raise money and troops during the French and Indian War. It did send one regiment, however, called the "Jersey Blues" because of the color of its uniforms.

Although New Jersey developed more slowly than some of the colonies, it became prosperous once the colonial wars ended. The settlers represented a number of different nationalities, and they were skilled in a good many different trades and occupations. The Dutch, Swedes and Finns were mostly farmers—thrifty and hard-working. The Quakers, too, were mainly farmers, but among them were shrewd businessmen and traders. The English settlers included many skilled craftsmen. Some who had come originally from New England were seafaring men. They settled on the coast and engaged in whaling and fishing.

Farming was by far the most important occupation. Large crops of wheat, corn, oats, flax and hemp were raised. Most farmers kept cattle, hogs, sheep and horses. Of somewhat less importance were the fur trade, fishing and whaling. Forest products included lumber, staves and shingles, as well as pitch and resin from the trees in the extensive pine forests in the central part of the colony.

New Jersey was never a great seafaring colony, but

it did find markets for its farm and forest products. A few New Jersey ships sailed direct to the West Indies and across the Atlantic. But Philadelphia, already a large seaport, was just across the Delaware River from southern New Jersey. New York was close to the northern part. Grain, flour, boards, shingles, staves, beef and pork could be shipped to these ports in small coastwise vessels and then reloaded into oceangoing ships.

Some of the towns along the shore flourished because of this trade. Burlington, on the Delaware, was the largest in southern New Jersey. Carts rattled on and off its wharf, and windlasses creaked aboard the craft lying there. Into the vessels went farm and forest products. Out of them came manufactured goods from Europe, as well as West Indian sugar, rum, dyewoods and tropical fruit. The same activity could be seen in northern towns along the Hudson and New York harbor.

There were other thriving places. Among them were Elizabeth, the largest settlement in the colony during the eighteenth century, and Newark, New Brunswick, Perth Amboy and Princeton.

Although New Jersey had little industry, its iron works were important. Ores rich in iron had been discovered in the northern part of the colony, and an iron mine was opened in 1665. Others were soon established.  Iron works were erected to smelt the ore.

Britain did everything it could to discourage manufacturing in America so that it could continue to sell its own manufactures there. Nevertheless, New Jersey defied the English efforts and was soon turning out articles made of iron. Primarily, though, it was an agricultural colony. Its rolling farmlands were the chief livelihood of the settlers.

# chapter 6

# *The Connecticut Colony*

A broad and beautiful river rises far to the north near Canada, flows down the middle of what is now the state of Connecticut and empties into Long Island Sound. The Indians appropriately called it the Connecticut, meaning "Long River." For many years, however, the settlers along its banks called it the Great River.

The soil of its valley, deposited by spring floods in bygone centuries, was so rich that almost any crops would grow in it. Its dense forests provided a limitless store of timber, and teemed with fur-bearing animals. Vast schools of shad and salmon swam up the river to spawn. Vessels of good size could sail a distance of fifty miles before reaching the first of its falls.

Thomas Hooker, pastor of the Puritan church of Newtown, now Cambridge, just outside Boston, had heard of the fertile valley to the west. Because of his

Puritan preachings in England, he had been hounded by the head of the Church of England, the Archbishop of Canterbury, and had fled to America. Instead of finding a haven where he could live in peace, Hooker found only disappointment in Newtown.

The austere ministers of Massachusetts Bay believed in strict enforcement of the rigid Puritan doctrines. Hooker did not agree. He began to think of taking his followers to a place where their lives would not be so harshly dominated by the church.

Others in Newtown were ready to go with him. In the summer of 1636, Hooker and about a hundred of these dissatisfied people set out. It was a difficult and hazardous journey. No roads led through the forested, hilly wilderness—not even a good trail. Yet the group set off, trudging patiently along and driving before them 160 head of lowing cattle and bawling calves, as well as squealing pigs and bleating goats. It was two weeks before they reached their goal.

They settled on the west bank of the Great River, a few miles below the first falls, calling the place Newtown. Later they renamed it Hartford. It was not the first settlement in Connecticut. In 1633 the Dutch of New Netherland had established a fur trading post a short distance above Hartford. That same year Englishmen from the Plymouth colony founded Windsor, at the falls. In 1635 three groups from Massachusetts

Bay settled along the river. One of the expeditions founded Wethersfield, a little below Hartford. Another settled close to Windsor. The third took possession of the river's mouth and started Saybrook.

Hartford became the most important settlement, however, because of Thomas Hooker. He united Hartford, Windsor and Wethersfield into the Connecticut colony and guided it wisely through its early years of hardship and of peril from the Indians.

However, there was friction between the Puritans and the settlers from Plymouth at Windsor. The Puritan group had settled almost next door to the Plymouth people without an invitation. Another source of trouble was the little Dutch trading post close to Hartford. Like two hostile dogs, these two settlements glowered at each other, though neither went so far as to start a fight. Finally, when the English seized New Netherland in 1664, they removed the threat from the Dutch settlers on the Great River.

The quarrels among colonists, however, were nothing like the fights waged with certain Indians. The Mohegans, who lived in the settled region of Connecticut, were friendly, but the Pequots to the east were a fierce and bloodthirsty tribe. They were determined to kill all the white settlers of Connecticut.

Time after time, the Pequots tried in vain to seize the fort at Saybrook. Then in 1637 they raided

Wethersfield, killed nine people and carried off two women. With that, Connecticut declared war.

The Pequot War was one of the smallest and shortest Indian battles fought in the American colonies. But it also proved to be a very bloody one. Captain John Mason, with a tiny army of 89 soldiers and about 80 Mohegan allies, sailed down the Great River to Long Island Sound. Then the party turned their three small ships east to Narragansett Bay, where they landed and obtained the help of about 500 Narragansett warriors. The Narragansetts were the enemies of the Pequots.

Mason's reinforced army then marched by land approximately 25 miles westward to the Pequots' stronghold. The Indian fort covered an acre or so of ground. It was surrounded by a stout stockade of tree trunks twelve feet high, set close together. Inside, in about 70 wigwams, were all the Pequot warriors. They probably numbered close to 600.

In the darkness, Mason's force crept stealthily to a well-concealed position near the fort. The Pequots, unaware that an enemy was near, were having a war dance. Until late at night the English sentries could hear them howling and screeching.

At dawn, Mason's army struck through two entrances on opposite sides of the fort. They took the sleeping warriors by surprise in the wigwams. Many fell before the attackers' musket balls and sword strokes as they tried to flee. The rest were burned to death when Mason's men set fire to the wigwams. In less than an hour the Pequots' power was utterly destroyed.

In the spring of 1638 another band of English colonists arrived on the Connecticut shore of Long Island Sound. They landed at a place which the Indians called Quinnipiac. Later the settlers changed its name to New Haven.

Their leader was a Puritan minister, John Davenport, who, like Thomas Hooker, had been persecuted in England. He had assembled some followers and sailed for Massachusetts Bay. Several towns there would have welcomed them as settlers, but some London merchants among the group wanted a place of their own with a good harbor.

From the first, New Haven did not get along with the other Connecticut settlements. Davenport was the strictest kind of Puritan. For years New Haven remained separate from the Connecticut colony. Like Massachusetts Bay, it was a theocracy. The Puritan church was all-powerful in its government, and its laws were based on those of the Bible, rather than the Common Law developed in England through centuries of experience.

These church laws were so harsh that a person who took part in any sort of game or sport on the Sabbath could be put to death. Persons of other faiths were not permitted to settle in New Haven. Although the government in Thomas Hooker's Connecticut colony was also a Puritan theocracy, it was much more liberal.

In contrast to most of the early American colonies, Connecticut had been settled without a royal charter. Massachusetts Bay had simply given Hooker permission to go to Connecticut, since it claimed that region. For a quarter of a century, Connecticut governed itself without any control by England.

More settlers were coming and new towns were being founded. The leaders decided the colony should have a charter of its own, especially since Massachusetts Bay wanted to annex it. They planned to ask that the New Haven colony be included in Connecticut under the charter. New Haven had by then spread out to include a number of other nearby towns.

New Haven fought the proposal bitterly. Perhaps it might have remained separate from the Connecticut colony if events hadn't taken an unexpected turn.

In 1649 Charles I of England was convicted of treason and beheaded. His execution marked the end of his 24-year struggle over power with the English Parliament. For Charles had believed in "the divine right of kings" to govern as they saw fit. His death also marked a temporary end to the struggle between aristocrats (Cavaliers) and Puritans (Roundheads) for control of England. Oliver Cromwell, the Puritan leader, became the ruler of England with the title of Protector.

By the time Cromwell died, in 1658, the English people were dissatisfied with the Protectorate. They invited Charles' son to return to the throne. Young Charles II began to take swift revenge against the Puritan judges who had signed his father's death warrant. Ten of these "regicides," as they were called, were hanged. Nineteen others received life imprisonment. The rest fled from England.

The King was especially anxious to catch and hang two of those who escaped. One was Edward Whalley, Cromwell's cousin. The other was Whalley's son-in-law, William Goffe. Both refugees had managed to get aboard a ship bound for Boston.

In March of 1661 a rumor flew from house to house in the settlement of New Haven:

"Two regicides are here!" the colonists whispered breathlessly to one another. Whalley and Goffe had come to New Haven, sure that such a staunch Puritan colony would protect them.

The Puritan leader and minister, John Davenport, gave them sanctuary in his house. But two royal agents

sent to Boston to catch them were already headed for
New Haven. Word of their approach reached the
town. Whalley and Goffe left Davenport's house and
hid in another house near by.

On the way to New Haven, the King's emissaries
stopped at Guilford, where the colony's deputy governor, William Leete, lived. He was as devout a Puritan as Davenport, and had no use for Charles II. He
said he had seen nothing of Whalley and Goffe. The
agents immediately wanted to set out for New Haven,
but Leete stopped them. He explained that it was
Saturday night. The Puritan Sabbath had begun. No
one was permitted to travel until it was over.

By the time the emissaries reached New Haven on
Monday, Whalley and Goffe had been warned. They
fled to a rocky hill on the outskirts of the town. There
they hid in a cave until the royal agents gave up their
search and went on to New Amsterdam, hoping to find
their quarry there. Today the "Judges' Cave" can still
be seen on West Rock in New Haven. Below it traffic
on a superhighway roars into a tunnel bored through
the hill.

Some historians believe Charles II was so angry at
New Haven's interference that he refused the colony's
plea to remain separate. Anyhow, when he issued
a charter in 1662, New Haven was made part of
Connecticut. In time its Puritan power was broken

and it became less bigoted toward settlers of other faiths.

The King's charter gave the Connecticut settlers great freedom in governing themselves; it also provided for their liberties as Englishmen. But unfortunately, Connecticut was still a Puritan colony. It could never match its liberties with those of Pennsylvania and Rhode Island, where settlers enjoyed complete religious freedom.

Connecticut again displayed its rugged spirit in 1687. After James II came to the English throne, he decided to revoke the charters of all American colonies which were still allowed to choose their own government. He planned to place them under royal governors.

Soon afterward tyrannical Andros arrived in Boston to become governor of all New England. The King's detested agent, Edward Randolph, was also there. Randolph sent an insolent letter to Connecticut, demanding the surrender of its charter. The Connecticut officials replied that the colony was perfectly satisfied with its government and preferred to keep the charter.

Andros then set out for Connecticut with 60 soldiers to enforce his bidding. In Hartford he was escorted to the meetinghouse, where the General Assembly was gathered.

It was late on a dreary October afternoon, and candles were lighted. Andros read his commission as royal governor of New England and asked for the charter. It was brought out and laid on the table. Suddenly all the candles were blown out. By the time they had been relighted, the charter had vanished.

Tradition has it that the charter was spirited away by a patriotic member of the Assembly and hidden in a certain ancient, gigantic, hollow oak tree. When the great oak finally fell in 1856 it was estimated to be 800 years old. Today, in the State House at Hartford, capital of the state of Connecticut, the governor's chair is made from the wood of the famous Charter Oak.

Connecticut could not prevent Andros from assuming power, but as soon as he was overthrown the colony established its old government, with all its liberties and privileges.

Again, in the colonial wars, Connecticut demonstrated its patriotism and a spirit of unity with its neighbor colonies. Although it was never seriously threatened during that half century of strife with the French, Connecticut sent more soldiers than any other colony to fight on the northern frontiers.

In a modest way, Connecticut prospered financially in these years of the eighteenth century. There was nothing modest about its growth, however. From 1701 to 1774 its population increased sixfold to nearly

200,000 people. It was one of the most densely popu-
lated colonies, especially the section along the shore of
Long Island Sound.

Most of the people were farmers. Connecticut exported some of its agricultural products to the West
Indies, but most of its trade was with neighboring
colonies. Tobacco grew well in the Connecticut River
valley. Although the crop was never as important to
Connecticut as to Virginia, some tobacco was exported.
Shipyards multiplied, and so did the ships. Mostly
they were small vessels for the coastal trade. As for
manufacturing, there was little. However, several iron
works were set up in western Connecticut when ore
was found there. A number of craftsmen turned out
fine clocks, starting an industry for which Connecticut
later became famous.

Connecticut was unique among the American colonies for the peaceful way in which it grew under its
government. This was probably because, except for
Andros' brief rule, it was never a royal province. The
colony chose its own governors. There were few quarrels between them and the Assembly. Connecticut
liked its governors and reelected some of them time
after time. Until the approach of the American Revolution, Connecticut might well have been called the
Peaceful Colony.

# chapter 7

# Lord Baltimore's Noble Venture

The Reformation, which began in England during the reign of Henry VIII, caused the disestablishment of the Catholic religion there. In its place the Protestant Church of England was established. Many devoted Catholics who refused to give up their faith were severely persecuted.

They found a great and powerful friend in George Calvert. He had been born a Protestant, but became a Catholic. In spite of this, the Protestant James I thought so well of Calvert that he knighted him as Lord Baltimore.

This first Lord Baltimore was heartsick over the stern English laws which made it impossible for Catholics to worship in peace and safety. He decided to find a haven in America for the afflicted people of the Church of Rome.

By that time Charles I had succeeded James I. Since he too was a Protestant, he might not have looked with favor on Baltimore's plan had his Queen not been a Catholic. She pleaded with Charles, and he granted Lord Baltimore land along Chesapeake Bay, north of Virginia. In the charter issued in 1632, the land was described as *Terra Mariae*—Maryland—after Queen Henrietta Maria.

No American colony ever received a better charter. The settlers were granted all the rights of free Englishmen. Lord Baltimore was appointed the lord Proprietary. Representatives elected by the people, together with Lord Baltimore, shared in the law-making. The colony was given the right forever to consent to any taxes imposed upon it.

Religion was not even mentioned in the charter. The colony's legislature and the lord Proprietary were to decide all such questions.

Unlike the bigoted Puritans of Massachusetts, Lord Baltimore did not intend that Maryland should have only the Catholic religion. He planned to let settlers of all faiths come there to worship as they pleased.

Lord Baltimore never saw the colony that resulted from his noble purpose. He died before the first settlers sailed from England in two ships, the *Ark* and the *Dove,* in 1633. His son Cecilius became the second Lord Baltimore and lord Proprietary of Maryland.

There were some 200 colonists. Almost all were Catholics, well-to-do and respectable. Two Jesuit priests came with them. Lord Baltimore remained in England to round up more settlers. In his place was his brother, Leonard Calvert, who was to be governor.

The smaller of the ships, the *Dove*, almost foundered in a violent storm. For several weeks it was separated from the *Ark*. Not until late in March, 1634, were the settlers near their destination in Chesapeake Bay.

Seeking a good place for their settlement, they sailed on up the Potomac River. Near the mouth of a smaller stream flowing into it, they landed and began to build the first Catholic settlement in America. They called it St. Mary's.

The Piscataway Indians, who had a village near by, were delighted to sell the land in exchange for hatchets, hoes and cloth. They had already decided to move, for they were threatened with destruction by the warlike, more powerful Susquehannocks to the north.

The Maryland settlers suffered no such hardships as those of their neighbor colony, Virginia. A large supply of food had been loaded aboard the *Ark* and *Dove*. Also, they arrived during spring planting time, so they were able to raise a large crop of corn in the cleared cornfields left by the departing Piscataways. Indeed, they had such a large fall crop that they shipped a good-sized cargo to New England, where it was exchanged for salt fish.

The colonists did not even have to put up houses immediately. They used the rude huts in the deserted Indian village until they could build more substantial dwellings. They did erect a guardhouse and a storehouse, and a large hut that had been occupied by a Piscataway chief served as the first church in Maryland.

Maryland's development was much like that of Virginia. It too was tidewater country, with gently flowing rivers which could be used as highways as far as the foothills of the mountains in the west. The soil was similar, well suited to raising tobacco.

For a number of years all went well. The nearest Indians were some distance away, and there was no trouble with them. Land was cleared, and plantations sprang up along the principal rivers, the Potomac, St. Mary's and Patuxent. Chesapeake Bay was a veritable treasure-trove of sea food, especially oysters and crabs. Near St. Mary's there was fine clay for making bricks, and many colonists replaced their hand-hewn wooden houses with sturdy brick ones.

New settlers flooded in. Because of the first Lord Baltimore's decision to welcome people of all faiths, Maryland became a haven for persecuted people. Yet this very act of tolerance and generosity soon brought **serious trouble to the colony.**

It began when a Virginia settler, William Claiborne, established a trading post on Kent Island, just off the eastern shore of Chesapeake Bay in Maryland. Since Virginia claimed the whole Chesapeake region, Lord Baltimore feared this was a move to take over all of his colony. He ordered his brother, Governor Calvert, to seize Kent Island.

A small war broke out between Maryland and the settlers of the island. Armed boats sent out by Calvert and Claiborne engaged in two bloody fights. News of the dispute reached the King, who finally decided Kent Island belonged to Lord Baltimore.

That might have ended the trouble. But some Puritans who had been banished from Virginia for trying to convert the "ungodly Virginians" to their own stern religion, decided to settle in Maryland. They were sure of a welcome in the tolerant colony established by Lord Baltimore.

At the mouth of the Severn River, just across Chesapeake Bay from Kent Island, the new arrivals founded the settlement of Providence. They showed no gratitude for Lord Baltimore's tolerance, however. Not only did they refuse to take an oath of allegiance to Maryland, but they set up their own government in Providence.

Since the Puritans hated and feared the Church of Rome, they were delighted at the trouble Claiborne was stirring up. They allied themselves with him, ready to help in a revolt against Maryland.

Meanwhile, in England, the Puritans had gained control of Parliament in their bitter struggle against Charles I. Captain Richard Ingle, a tobacco trader who some claim was little better than a pirate, took his armed ship, the *Reformation,* to the Chesapeake.

Ingle landed a force at St. Mary's, took the fort there and seized control of Maryland in the name of the Parliament. The ungrateful Puritans joyously aided him. Governor Calvert had to flee to Virginia for safety.

Worse troubles were in the offing. When the Puritan Parliament triumphed in its civil war with Charles I and he was beheaded, Maryland and Virginia remained loyal to the Crown. Parliament sent a warship and forced the two colonies to yield. Claiborne gained his revenge at last. As one of the commissioners appointed by Parliament to rule Maryland, he had a strong voice in the colony which had taken Kent Island away from him.

For more than three years there was nothing but disorder in Maryland. The colony had no real government. Ingle had sailed away, but the fort at St. Mary's was occupied by his soldiers. They joined the Protestant servants of the Catholic landowners in wrecking the plantations and persecuting all Catholics. They

stripped the houses of all they contained, and stole grain and livestock. Jesuit priests were sent in chains to England, where they were imprisoned. The Catholic settlers lived in a state of fear.

For three years, Maryland was a Puritan colony, but while Oliver Cromwell ruled England as Protector, Lord Baltimore managed to get into his good graces. Cromwell gave Maryland back to him in 1658.

Some years after the Restoration in England, James II tried to bring the Catholic Church back to power. This, of course, helped to lead to his downfall. And once he was ousted, supporters of the Church of England in Maryland came into control of the colony. They asked the new rulers of England, William and Mary, to take Maryland away from Lord Baltimore again.

This was done, and Maryland became a royal province. The Church of England, or the Episcopal Church as it was now called in Maryland, became the official church of the colony. The Catholics were once more oppressed and persecuted. A tax to support the Episcopal ministers was levied upon Puritans, Catholics and Episcopalians alike. Colonists were forbidden to hold Catholic services. Quaker meetings, too, were declared unlawful, and Puritans were deprived of the rights all settlers had been granted under Maryland's charter.

So many Catholics fled that those who remained no longer had any power in the colony's Assembly. Many of the wealthier Catholic plantation owners who stayed built concealed chapels in their houses, where services could be held in secret.

The Episcopal-controlled Assembly decided on still more punishment for the Catholics, most of whom lived in or near St. Mary's. The Assembly removed the colony's capital to Providence, and its name was changed to Annapolis. As for St. Mary's, its population grew smaller and smaller until at last it was deserted, its houses toppling into ruin.

Even when King George I restored Maryland to the fourth Lord Baltimore, in 1715, the Catholics still did not regain their full rights. Fortunately the first Lord Baltimore did not live long enough to see the hatred and bigotry displayed by those who had taken advantage of his tolerance. He never knew how they had ruined his dream of a colony where those of all faiths could live and worship in harmony.

In spite of all this unhappiness, Maryland became a thriving colony. Tobacco was its chief product. True, the crop brought troubles, as it had to Virginia. When too much tobacco was raised and the price fell, there was distress. Slavery also put its dreadful curse upon the colony. But still tobacco remained Maryland's fortune, and by far her most important export. There were other sources of income, however—furs, wheat, flour, pork, beef and forest products. For home use the colonists tanned leather to make shoes. They set up several furnaces and forges which turned out nails and other iron manufactures.

New towns were rising up—Frederick, Georgetown (now part of the national capital of Washington) and Baltimore, destined to become a great metropolis and seaport. Settlers moved farther and farther west into the mountains.

Even the colonial wars did not threaten Maryland's progress at first, for it was in little danger during the earlier conflicts. Other colonies more immediately threatened thought that prosperous Maryland should help with food, money and soldiers, but the settlers on the Chesapeake did little until the French and Indian War.

Then the people were thrown into a panic when the French defeated Braddock so disastrously. Many settlers on the wilderness frontier fled to the safety of Baltimore. Annapolis began to fortify itself lest the French forces strike eastward. The colonists raised money and sent soldiers against the enemy. The capture of Fort Du Quesne finally destroyed the French menace.

The story of Maryland's rise to prosperity is much like that of Virginia, because its resources were so similar. The important difference is that the noble purpose of its founder was lost in years of strife and the persecution of its Catholic settlers. Yet even as these troubles continued, the people gradually learned that such bigotry did not benefit a colony. When religious persecution was done away with under the constitution of the new nation, the United States of America, Maryland readily joined the other twelve colonies in ratifying the action.

chapter 8

# The Smallest of Them All

There are several reasons why Rhode Island was different from the other American colonies. For one, because it was squeezed in among Massachusetts Bay, Plymouth and Connecticut, Rhode Island was the smallest colony, just as it is now the smallest state. Also, for two years it had only one settler. William Blackstone, a minister of the Church of England, was dissatisfied not only with the ways of that church, but also with those of other human beings. He left England in 1623 and was the first and only settler of Shawmut, which later became Boston. When the Puritan colonists arrived there in 1630, Blackstone left. He journeyed through the wilderness to what is now Rhode Island and settled down once more to his hermit's life.

His lonely cabin can scarcely be called a settlement.

The first real village came into existence six years later when another unusual man followed Blackstone to that region. It is not easy to know and understand Roger Williams because his character was so complex. He was pious and kind-hearted, with a deep compassion for the sufferings of persecuted people. At the same time he was obstinate, forever arguing and quarreling over the principles he believed in.

Williams was a Separatist minister who left England because he was persecuted. He came first to Massachusetts Bay. He was dissatisfied with what he found there, but he did not want to leave. For a time he served as assistant minister in the church at Salem. But he soon got into disputes with the Puritan ministers of Massachusetts Bay and left to become assistant minister at Plymouth.

During that time, Williams took a keen interest in the Indians and became the trusted friend of the great chief Massasoit. He went among the tribes, including the Narragansetts to the west, and learned the Indian language.

When the Salem church recalled him as its minister, his old troubles soon cropped up. The Puritan ministers were furious when Williams declared the church should have nothing to do with government. They were enraged too when he said no civil court should punish offenses like blasphemy and breaking the stern laws about observing the Sabbath, because they were offenses against God, not men.

Roger Williams did not want to be involved in these difficulties. When he found himself in court to explain why he had written that the King could not grant land in America because it belonged to the Indians, he was penitent and apologized. But in his heart he believed he was right. Williams' trouble was that he was always at war with his conscience. No matter how hard he tried, it would not let him stop upholding his beliefs.

At last the General Court banished him from Massachusetts Bay, but it did not wish to be cruel. Since winter was coming on, he was allowed to put off his departure until spring.

Williams went right on with his disputes. Finally, the General Court decided it must be rid of him at once. A ship was sent from Boston to Salem with orders to seize Williams and take him back to England.

Before the vessel could arrive, friends warned Roger Williams of the order. He left his wife and children in Salem and set out alone into the wilderness. It was early January, 1636, in a bitter winter.

Williams reached Massasoit's village. The friendly Wampanoags sheltered and fed him until spring. By that time several of his friends had joined him. They left the Indian village and settled on the Seekonk River, which flows into Narragansett Bay.

Puritan malevolence still followed Williams. His friend Governor Edward Winslow of Plymouth sent him a letter saying his settlement was on Plymouth property. The Pilgrim colony did not actually object to his being there, but it feared to offend powerful Massachusetts Bay by harboring the man the Puritans had outlawed.

Williams and his friends abandoned their settlement and paddled down the river in a canoe. They reached a cove on a peninsula between two rivers flowing into Narragansett Bay. After paying the Indians a fair price for their land, they began to build their new settlement. They named it Providence.

They had picked an excellent site. Because of its location on a hill, it was dry and well drained. Near by was a spring of sparkling water. The bay abounded in seafood and provided an excellent harbor. Tall oaks and cedars furnished timber to build the houses. There was plenty of game in the forests surrounding Providence.

Other Separatists, tired of Puritan harshness in Massachusetts Bay, soon migrated to Providence. With them came Williams' wife and children. A town was laid out, with houses built on ten-acre lots along a "Towne Street."

Williams wanted his colony to set an example of freedom and tolerance. It was founded upon the great principles in which he believed so firmly. The church was to be separate from the government. Land was to be obtained only by a fair purchase from the Indians, and no one was to be barred because of his religion.

As had happened in Maryland, religious tolerance permitted some troublemakers to come. One of them was William Coddington, a rich Boston merchant and a follower of Mrs. Ann Hutchinson. When Mrs. Hutchinson was banished from Massachusetts Bay, Williams offered her a refuge in his colony. He even bargained with the Indians for land on Aquidneck Island where she and her people could settle.

Aquidneck Island lies in the wide-open jaws of vast Narragansett Bay, like a fish about to be swallowed by a larger one. Here Mrs. Hutchinson, with Coddington and others, came in 1638 to a place with the Indian name of Pocasset. Later they renamed it Portsmouth.

Coddington, the real leader, was ambitious, quarrelsome, and he could be treacherous. His ways caused disputes among the Portsmouth settlers. In 1639 some of them moved farther south on the island and founded Newport.

A far worse mischief-maker was Samuel Gorton, leader of another religious sect. His insolence and his barbed tongue earned him the name of "Firebrand of New England." When Massachusetts Bay banished him, he came to Portsmouth. There Gorton set about to cause Coddington's downfall. At length he was summoned before the settlement's magistrates for some offense. Instead of addressing them as "Mr. Justice," he used the term "Mr. Just Ass." For that he was publicly whipped and told to leave.

The kindly and tolerant Roger Williams welcomed Gorton to Providence, but he soon caused so much trouble that he and his people were forced to leave. They went to Shawomet, south of Providence, and founded their settlement, which became Warwick.

For some years each of the four settlements—Providence, Portsmouth, Newport and Warwick—governed itself without interference from any other colony or from England. Roger Williams hoped to unite them, however. He realized that otherwise they might be swallowed, one at a time, by other New England colonies.

In 1643 Williams went to England to ask for a royal charter. It was granted in 1644 under the name of the Incorporation of Providence Plantations on the Narragansett Bay in New England.

The charter was very liberal. It gave the colony power to govern itself by electing a president and a General Assembly of four assistants, one from each settlement. Williams might easily have been the first president, but he was modestly content to be an assistant.

All seemed well, but Coddington was secretly plotting to separate the two Aquidneck settlements from the others. He went to England and in March, 1661, obtained a separate charter. Williams traveled to London right after him and protested strongly. He won out. Coddington was removed from his office and Portsmouth and Newport accepted the charter.

Roger Williams' colony had no trouble while Cromwell ruled, for the Protector was tolerant both in matters of religion and government. And when Charles II was restored to the throne, he granted the colony a new charter as liberal as the old one. It was issued in the name of the Colony of Rhode Island and Providence Plantations. Gradually it became known simply as Rhode Island, a name Roger Williams had given to Aquidneck Island.

Even under Governor Andros, affairs went smoothly. The despotic governor took a kindly attitude toward the colony, and no serious attempt was made to obtain the surrender of its charter.

Rhode Island suffered little during King Philip's War, because of Roger Williams' just treatment of the Indians. But the most important battle of the war, the Great Swamp Fight, took place there. And King Philip himself died in one of the colony's swamps.

As time passed, Rhode Island's religious toleration attracted many new settlers. They included Quakers and members of other sects. There were quarrels over religious issues, but Roger Williams had a powerful influence in guiding Rhode Island through every threat to its peace and good government.

Williams did not like Quakers. Because they refused to show respect for higher authority, even the King, he thought them uncivil and discourteous. Yet his conscience would not let him hate or discriminate against them.

Jews, who for centuries had been unjustly persecuted and hated, came to Rhode Island. Some had wandered from Europe to Brazil and then to New Amsterdam, which in turn banished them. Between 1655 and 1657 some of them settled in Newport and built the first synagogue in America. They were of distinguished Spanish-Portuguese families and made excellent colonists and citizens.

Roger Williams' great principles worked well, for Rhode Island grew and flourished. When he died in 1683 the colony was a shining example of religious toleration. And just before the Revolution the General Assembly did something he would have liked. Though there were few slaves in Rhode Island, the Assembly freed all of them and abolished slavery forever.

Rhode Island prospered, first of all, because of its farms. Along the coast, however, many people engaged in fishing. The colony also had iron ore and, in spite of all Britain's attempts to discourage manufacturing, several furnaces and forges were established. One made anchors, another nails, and a third produced axes, plows, hoes and other implements.

Since Narragansett Bay boasted several excellent harbors, Rhode Island produced seafaring men as skilled and bold as those of Massachusetts. In the early eighteenth century a number of shipyards were turning out vessels, large and small. Rhode Island shipped its agricultural and forest products to the West Indies and to American colonies as far south as the Carolinas in return for products it needed.

Rhode Island's part in the colonial wars was carried out very largely on the sea. Since there was no colonial navy, Rhode Island ships were armed and fitted out as privateers. All through these wars, these privateers sailed on marauding voyages against French sea trade. They took many valuable prizes; indeed, one Rhode Island privateer captured 23 enemy merchantmen on a single cruise.

For its size, Rhode Island also contributed more to the fighting on land than any other American colony. The tiny province raised men and money all through the years of strife. In the French and Indian war it sent more than 2,500 soldiers to the battlegrounds, though it was never threatened by French or Indian land forces.

Rhode Island's proudest heritage is that it was one of only two American colonies where settlers had full freedom to worship as they pleased. Others tried, but only Rhode Island and Pennsylvania succeeded. Tiny Rhode Island takes pride too in the fact that it achieved success in the face of difficulties and hardships much like those of other New England provinces. "Small but mighty" would be an apt description of little Rhode Island.

# chapter 9

# How Delaware Began

When Peter Stuyvesant came to New Amsterdam he was determined to keep what is now Delaware as a part of New Netherland. He also intended to drive out the Swedes and Finns who had made the first permanent settlement there.

Actually, the Dutch themselves were chiefly responsible for that settlement. A Dutchman named William Usselinx had realized that Sweden was anxious to join other European countries in colonizing the New World. So he had gone to Sweden and obtained a charter under which a company headed by Swedes and Dutchmen was organized. He then got in touch with Peter Minuit and hired him as director of the expedition.

Two vessels, the *Key of Kalmar* and the *Bird Griffin,* carried about 50 Swedish emigrants to Delaware Bay, arriving late in March, 1638. They sailed on up the Delaware River to the mouth of a smaller stream flowing into it. This they called Christina Creek after the young Queen of Sweden. Their colony, of course, was to be named New Sweden.

A short distance up the creek they landed at a place they called The Rocks. Here they began to build their settlement. Peter Minuit bought the land from the Indians who lived in the neighborhood. Though he failed to make quite as profitable a deal as his purchase of Manhattan Island, it was nevertheless a good one. Today Wilmington, Delaware's largest city and a great industrial center, stands there.

First the settlers built a square log fort with two log houses inside it. There they could safely store their goods and provisions. Then they laid out their village, which they named Christina.

Word of the New Sweden colony reached Governor Kieft in New Netherland. He sent an angry protest to Peter Minuit. The land belonged to New Netherland, he said, and he warned that the Swedes must get out. Minuit paid no attention.

A new governor of New Sweden was appointed in 1639. Peter Minuit sailed for Holland, but his ship foundered in a hurricane and the man who had bought Manhattan Island for twenty-four dollars was lost with her.

The Swedish government now began to find it difficult to obtain more colonists for Christina. At last it took strong measures to provide them. All married soldiers who had deserted the army or committed other serious offenses were ordered to America with their families.

Then 32 Finns who had left their own country and had come uninvited to Sweden were asked to go to America. When they refused, they were seized and sent to New Sweden despite their protests. They made valuable settlers, for among them were carpenters, shipbuilders, blacksmiths, farmers and sailors. Their skills were of great importance to the colony. The Swedish government also granted permission for about twenty Dutch families to come to Christina.

Soon word spread through Sweden that the land along the Delaware was rich and excellent for farming. The Swedish government had less difficulty finding people to go to America. In 1642 a new governor, Johan Printz, was appointed. He sailed with three ships carrying arms and ammunition. The convoy also transported goods needed in the colony, as well as a large number of settlers, many of them farmers.

Although Printz was coarse and domineering, he had a great deal of energy and the ability to get things done. Under his administration, New Sweden continued to grow and prosper. Three more expeditions arrived bringing colonists.

Some of these settled on the New Jersey side of the Delaware. This angered the Dutch still more. Peter Stuyvesant, as governor of New Netherland, retaliated by building Fort Casimir on the west side of the Delaware River. Now it was the Swedes' turn to protest. But the Dutch simply ignored them.

Then Johan Rising was sent from Sweden to replace Printz. He had orders to drive the Dutch from the west side of the Delaware.

Rising arrived in a Swedish warship with 250 new settlers and 50 soldiers. When he demanded Fort Casimir's surrender, the garrison yielded and the Swedish flag replaced that of Holland. The Dutch commander and most of his soldiers took an oath of allegiance to Sweden and were allowed to stay.

Finally Stuyvesant himself went after the colony with a fleet of seven ships and 600 men. It was his intention to clear the Swedes from the New Jersey side of the river as well as from the west. The campaign took ten days, but it succeeded. The Dutch became the masters of New Sweden. As a result, the Swedes had to take an oath of allegiance to Holland if they wanted to remain.

The Dutch began to strengthen their hold on their conquest. They laid out a new town near Fort Casimir and called it New Amstel after the River Amstel,

which flows through Amsterdam in Holland. In the spring of 1657 three ships brought 167 Dutch colonists to settle there.

The Dutch had no more luck in holding onto their conquest than the Swedes. After the surrender of New Amsterdam to the English, Sir Robert Carr sailed toward the Delaware colony with two warships and a force of soldiers. The British expedition arrived at New Amstel on September 30, 1664.

Carr massed his troops on shore, ready for an attack. The cannon aboard his frigates thundered in two broadsides, sending balls smashing into flimsy Fort Casimir. Then the soldiers stormed and took the garrison.

The settlements on the west shore of Delaware Bay and the river became English under the rule of New York. English they remained until the American Revolution. New Amstel was renamed New Castle. It became the principal town of the colony.

Another change soon came. William Penn had bought West New Jersey and the first Quaker settlement had been founded there, but he needed more land for his persecuted people. Charles II granted him land on the west side of the Delaware River. The King, however, was mindful of New York's conquest. So he carefully left the region along the lower part of the river and bay out of the grant. "Except the three lower counties," was the way the charter read. These counties are now the state of Delaware.

William Penn, shrewd and wise, did not like this arrangement. He planned that his settlement of Philadelphia on the west shore of the Delaware River should become a great city and seaport. The three lower counties were a threat to his plan. The growing town of New Castle was planted like a watchful bulldog on the shore of the river a good 25 miles below the site he had chosen for Philadelphia. Ships coming up from the sea would reach New Castle first. It might easily rob Philadelphia of the sea trade which would make it great.

Penn found a way to avoid that. He asked James, the Duke of York, to give the three lower counties to him. The Duke did so. This enabled the Quaker leader to make sure that Philadelphia, not New Castle, became a great seaport.

When William Penn sailed for America in 1682 with settlers for his new colony of Pennsylvania, the ships put in first at New Castle. The English, Dutch and Swedish settlers gave him a warm welcome and promised obedience. A little later they presented a petition to Penn asking that he annex the colony to Pennsylvania. This Penn did.

But the people soon regretted their hasty request. They began to feel they were being treated as a stepchild of Penn's larger and more powerful colony. Unlike the plan which had been adopted when the two parts of New Jersey were united, the combined Assembly of Penn's merged colonies met only in Philadelphia. And what later became the state of Delaware was known only as the "three lower counties of Pennsylvania."

The Delaware settlers had an even bigger grievance. Penn was supposed to have promised that all ships sailing in and out of Delaware Bay should be entered and cleared at New Castle. In this way the lower counties could obtain revenues from the charges made for entrance and clearance. And once the ships were at New Castle they might find it convenient to load and unload cargo there.

Actually, most ships coming in and out of Delaware Bay were using Philadelphia. It was rapidly becoming one of the great seaports of America, while the wharves at New Castle were almost deserted. Delaware claimed that Penn had broken his promise.

In 1691 the lower counties' anger boiled over. Six of their members in the Assembly met secretly, organized a separate Council and passed some laws for the lower counties. Their quarrel with Pennsylvania continued until 1704, when the first independent assembly met at New Castle. But although Delaware was allowed to have its own Assembly, it had the same governor and Council as Pennsylvania. Until the Revolution this separate yet not separate arrangement continued.

The colonial wars had now begun. Although Delaware was not greatly threatened during the earlier ones, it raised troops and supplied provisions for the colonial army. When the Middle Colonies were menaced during the French and Indian War, the three lower counties raised forty companies to fight the French.

Delaware's population and prosperity grew rapidly in the eighteenth century. Although it could not hope to rival Pennsylvania's busy industry, many gristmills and sawmills were built along the colony's streams. It also had several iron forges.

Some of the original Swedish and Finnish settlers were seafaring men. They, and in turn their descendants, became expert pilots, guiding ships up and down the bay and river. There was considerable shipbuilding at Wilmington, which had first been called Christina. But the most important occupation was farming.

Delaware provided fine farming country. The colonists raised large crops of grain, flax, vegetables and fruit. Herds of livestock grazed in its grassy meadows. Much produce was shipped to market in

Philadelphia.

Like New Jersey, Delaware was primarily an agricultural colony. In later years, however, it achieved importance in industry, as well as in the shipping trade which Pennsylvania had captured in colonial days. The people were quite content with their farms and their colony's modest prosperity—even while they resented being a neglected part of Pennsylvania. If the settlers had not been fiercely independent they might in time have been completely absorbed by the more powerful colony. Then there would have been no Delaware, and just twelve states would have formed the new nation when it came into being.

# chapter 10

# William Penn's Holy Experiment

Pennsylvania may lay claim to being the tenth of the thirteen American colonies. In 1643 the Swedes who settled Delaware also established a trading post and settlement on an island in the Delaware River near the mouth of the Schuylkill River. The post was within the boundaries of what is now Pennsylvania.

Not until 1681, however, did the first Quakers come to settle William Penn's colony, which had been named Pennsylvania. Penn called this haven for his persecuted people his "holy experiment." Like Rhode Island and Maryland, it was planned as a place where people of all religious faiths might worship freely.

William Penn had experienced severe persecution. But being a man of great courage and determination, he had successfully resisted it. When the Bishop of London offered him a choice of giving up his religion or being imprisoned for life, Penn replied, "My prison shall be my grave before I will budge a jot." Then he wrote a pamphlet defending himself. It reached King Charles II, who was so impressed that he released Penn.

Again he was arrested. Since he was a lawyer, Penn acted as his own counsel when the case came to trial. So convincing were his arguments that he was found innocent in spite of an intolerant judge who had ordered the jury to convict him. Such was the man who founded Pennsylvania.

Charles II granted Penn land for his colony on the west side of the Delaware River. Penn wanted to call this colony New Wales, for he had heard that the country was a good deal like Wales in Britain. But the King did not care for this name. Then Penn suggested Sylvania, which means "woodland," but the King insisted on adding "Penn" before it.

Penn himself decided on the name for his first settlement in Pennsylvania. His reason for choosing Philadelphia, meaning "brotherly love," was that he intended it to be just that kind of a city.

Penn sent an advance party of colonists in the fall of 1681 to select a proper site. He told them to choose it with great care. It must be high and dry, yet near the Delaware River at a place where there was a good deep channel for ships.

In the spring of 1682, Penn sent a surveyor to lay out Philadelphia. Unlike Boston and New York, where the streets wound about haphazardly, and even followed cowpaths, the new settlement was to have broad, straight ones. Penn ordered the surveyor to take care that the houses had room on each side "for gardens, orchards or fields, that it may be a green country town that will never be burned and always wholesome."

Penn drew up a set of laws for the colony. Known as the Charter of Liberties, it could stand beside Maryland's royal charter as a splendid foundation for freedom, tolerance and good government. Pennsylvania was to have a governor (Penn was proprietor and the first governor) and a lieutenant governor. For making laws, both a Council and an Assembly would be elected by the people. The governor had the power to appoint judges, preside over the Council and veto laws of which he disapproved.

All colonists who owned land and believed in God could vote. No one was to be discriminated against or molested because of his religion. In England at that time there were some two hundred offenses—including the theft of a loaf of bread—for which a person could be hanged. In Pennsylvania only those who committed murder or treason could be deprived of their lives.

With more than a hundred colonists, Penn left Eng-

land in the 300-ton ship *Welcome*. Disaster threatened to wipe out all the passengers when a smallpox epidemic swept the vessel and a third of the passengers died. The survivors sailed into Delaware Bay on October 27, 1682.

Penn was enchanted with the land he saw as the white-winged *Welcome* sailed on up the bay and river. There were broad meadows, and beyond them the trackless forest in all the splendor of its autumn foliage. "The air smelled as sweet as a garden new blown," Penn later wrote.

Ten houses and a combination trading post and tavern had already been put up on the high bank above the river. The new colonists immediately set to work to build their homes. There were men of various trades and professions among them, including carpenters. Some were rich, some poor, but all were free—most of them for the first time in their lives.

Almost at once Penn made friends and a lasting peace with the Lenni-Lenapes or Delaware Indians who lived around Philadelphia. He abided by the Golden Rule, "Do unto others as you would be done by," and used it with the Indians. "Don't abuse them, but let them have justice and you will win them," he told his people. White settlers in America violated many a treaty with the Indians, but Penn's pact of love and friendship was never broken as long as the

Quakers controlled Pennsylvania.

With his colony established, Penn wanted more settlers. In 1684 he returned to England and worked constantly to get people to come to Pennsylvania. He was probably the first American colonist to understand the value of advertising. Advertise he did, with pamphlets describing the beauty and richness of Pennsylvania and the good fortune it promised to settlers.

These were distributed in England, Wales, Scotland, Ireland, Holland and Germany. Penn also had agents in these countries to sign up immigrants. To those who were well-to-do he offered 50 acres of land for each indentured servant they brought with them. Each servant was offered 50 acres as soon as he paid off what he owed his master.

Penn was determined that Pennsylvania should have none of the great landowners or the land speculation which had brought such trouble to New York. Land was sold in moderate-sized parcels to settlers only.

Colonists flocked to Pennsylvania. The wisdom of making a colony a "melting pot" of many nationalities had already been proved in New York. Pennsylvania was even more attractive to the downtrodden and persecuted people of Europe. It contained no great landowners to hold their tenants under oppression. And religious persecution was unknown.

Only 18 years after its settlement, Philadelphia had

10,000 people. Soon it outstripped Boston as the largest city in America. The whole colony was spreading westward very rapidly. Between 1682 and 1700, Pennsylvania's population multiplied itself 40 times, to a total of 20,000.

In and around Philadelphia, the southeastern part of the colony, lived the Quakers, Welsh and other English settlers. They were the merchants, skilled craftsmen and such professional men as doctors and lawyers.

Other new immigrants sought homes in the broad valleys west of the earlier settlements near the Delaware River. They were the Germans, Dutch and Swiss, almost all of them farmers. The soil of this region was ideal for growing a great variety of crops.

Many of these settlers were Amish or Mennonite, or belonged to other religious sects. They were mostly Germans, but because *Deutsch* is the word for German in their language, they became known as "Pennsylvania Dutch." They were expert farmers, hard working and thrifty. Their farms were models of excellence. They made this region one of the best areas for general farming in America.

Scotch-Irish immigrants, who were victims of religious persecution in Ireland, preferred to push west through the rugged wilderness, settling beyond the Allegheny Mountains. Among them were traders and trappers. They came into conflict with the French from Canada, who were also determined to capture the rich fur trade.

The great leaders of the colony were the Quakers. Like Penn, they lived by the Golden Rule, were honest, frugal and hard-working. At the same time their shrewd business sense made them successful merchants and traders. Philadelphia was the center for this trade, and the city and its wharves boomed with activity.

During his stay in England, which lasted 15 years, Penn had a good deal of trouble. When William and Mary came to the throne, they suspected he was plotting to restore the deposed James II. In 1692 Penn's governorship was taken away from him. Governor Benjamin Fletcher's rule of New York was extended to include Pennsylvania. Penn finally convinced William and Mary of his loyalty, however, and he was restored as governor in 1694.

Penn came back to his colony in 1699, but soon there was a movement in England to revoke the charters of all American colonies and place them directly under the Crown. He went back in 1701 to fight for Pennsylvania's right to govern itself.

Before he left he revised his Charter of Liberties. It was known as the Charter of Privileges, and it gave the people even greater freedom in governing themselves. In 1751, to commemorate the fiftieth anniversary of the Charter of Privileges, a great bell was hung in Carpenters' Hall in Philadelphia. It would later become forever famous as the Liberty Bell.

Nothing came of the threat to Pennsylvania's charter, but new troubles beset Penn in England. Due to the dishonesty of his business secretary, he found himself owing thousands of pounds. He could pay only part of the debt. At last he was forced to go into one of the terrible debtors' prisons in London.

Penn's wife and some of his Quaker friends raised the money to pay the rest of the debt, and he was released. But he was a ruined man. He had to sell his proprietorship of Pennsylvania to the Crown. He insisted, however, that the people of the colony must keep all the rights his charter had granted them.

Before the sale could be completed, Penn was paralyzed by a stroke. His mind was affected, but he lingered on for six years until 1718, when he died.

Penn's "holy experiment" had worked well. Only one other colony—Rhode Island—could match it for tolerance and freedom from religious persecution. Pennsylvania's people enjoyed more privileges and self-government than any other. Although the Quaker colony had existed only 36 years, it was well on its way to surpassing much older ones in prosperity and population.

Penn's three sons took over as proprietors of the colony. They did not have their father's gift for getting along with the Indians. Soon William Penn's treaty of friendship was endangered for the first time because of the "Walking Purchases."

Early deeds to land bought from the Indians often measured the extent of the purchase as the amount a man could walk around in a day and a half. Under the younger Penns the Indians were often cheated unmercifully when land was bought in this way. Men were trained to walk at great speed and sometimes relays of them were used to cover an immense amount of ground.

This angered the Indians at the very time when their friendship was most needed. Although Pennsylvania was not menaced by the French until the French and Indian War began in 1755, its frontier settlements were endangered by the Indians all through the colonial wars. And Pennsylvania was weak and unprepared for attack.

This weakness stemmed from the Quakers, whose religion forbade them to take part in wars. The Quaker-controlled Assembly ignored appeals from other colonies which were in danger. It refused to raise militia or fortify Pennsylvania's frontier.

While King George's War was being fought, New England sent an urgent appeal for aid. The Assembly would provide no soldiers, guns or ammunition, but it did appropriate money for food. This was described as "wheat and other grain." Governor George Thomas, who was not a Quaker, said it was plain that "other grain" must mean grains of powder. He bought some and sent it to New England.

Another great early Pennsylvanian, Benjamin Franklin, found an alternate solution to the Quakers' pacifism. This wise and brilliant man was no Quaker, and he saw clearly Pennsylvania's peril. During King George's War he organized his own corps of militia, and 10,000 men volunteered, though there was no immediate danger to the colony.

Pennsylvania was greatly menaced, however, during the French and Indian War. When Braddock was defeated in the far western part of Pennsylvania, the Delaware Indians struck, raiding the frontier. The people of the eastern towns became terrified that the French and the Indians might advance against them. The Quakers lost their control of the Assembly. The colony raised money for defense, and a chain of forts was erected along the frontier. That marked the end of the Quakers' rule, although they continued as a good and a powerful influence in the colony.

Pennsylvania stands among the most prosperous of the American colonies. It owes this high rank to the leadership, wisdom and shrewd business ability of its founder, William Penn. He believed in and practiced a precept that is found among his writings: "The public must and will be served."

# chapter 11

# The First of the Carolinas

In some ways North Carolina was much like its neighbor Virginia. It too had a tidewater region or coastal plain, a piedmont or plateau to the west, and a mountainous section beyond that. Like Virginia it had a number of good-sized rivers flowing into the ocean. In a large area the soil was excellent for growing fine tobacco.

For the most part, however, North Carolina's rivers could not be used as highways for trade. Along most of its coastline, North Carolina was rimmed by a chain of long, narrow islands. Between them and the mainland were sounds in which the water was shallow. Thus it was difficult for ships of any size to enter the rivers from the sea.

Another important difference between Virginia and her southern neighbor was the way North Carolina was colonized. The first permanent settlements, unlike those of most other American colonies, were not made by people from overseas. Colonists spread slowly into the North Carolina region from Virginia, beginning about 1653.

By 1663 a number of Virginians were living in the northeastern corner of what is now North Carolina, mostly along the Albemarle River. In that year Charles II paid off a debt he owed to eight prominent Englishmen who had aided him in recovering his throne. He granted the region south of Virginia to them as proprietors of "Carolina," named in his honor.

In England, the proprietors tried hard to get people to come to Carolina. They offered a hundred acres of land free. Settlers were to pay no taxes for a year. Traders from other colonies were not allowed to deal with the Indians. Quitrents, the small charges paid to the proprietors each year, were no higher than those in Virginia.

As for government, the people were to elect representatives to an Assembly. This body, along with a governor and council appointed by the proprietors, was to make the laws and have other important powers. The colonists were to enjoy all the rights of Englishmen and were not to be taxed without their consent.

Few settlers came, however. The soil was good, the

forests teemed with fur animals, and the streams and Albemarle Sound with fish. But the region was a great wilderness, cut off from easy communication with the other colonies. Trade from the sea was hampered by the shallow sound and the island chain beyond. And there were no roads between the colony and its neighbors to the north.

Then in 1669 the proprietors tried to set up a new kind of government in Albemarle County, as the settled area was called. It was a feudal type of system which tended to enslave the people, and it did not work. The colonists were rough, strong-willed men. Because they were true pioneers who had left the flourishing Virginia settlements to battle the wilderness, they had a fierce independence.

They did not like the governors sent to rule them. One was forced to flee. The people deposed another. Armed men seized a third and threw him in jail, and a fourth was banished. During this time the county was a lawless region with no real government.

Meanwhile, the proprietors had become interested in colonizing the far southern part of Charles' grant. In 1691, they appointed a governor of Carolina who lived at Charles Town. This was a settlement in the region that would one day be South Carolina. It was impossible for delegates from Albemarle County to attend the sessions of the Assembly in Charles Town, some 300 miles away. Therefore Albemarle County had its own Assembly, and also a deputy governor to rule it.

For the next 15 years the deputy governors were capable men of fine character and sound judgment. The northern part of Carolina enjoyed an orderly, efficient and peaceful government. It was as though the oppressive feudal system had been a dam blocking off a flood of settlement. Now it had burst, and a veritable wave of new settlers swept in.

First came French Huguenots from Virginia. They settled along the Pamlico River, south of Albemarle. More Huguenots from Virginia ventured farther south, along the Neuse and Trent rivers. By 1694 the colony's population was about 3,000.

The first settlers from Europe came from London. Except for a few Englishmen, however, they were Germans and some Swiss who had been driven from their homelands by persecution. They settled New Bern on the Neuse River.

All might have continued to go well with the colony but for the largest and most warlike of the many Indian tribes, the Tuscaroras. In dealing with the Indians, the settlers had used none of the fairness and understanding of such colonies as Pennsylvania and Rhode Island. They simply took the land. For years, traders cheated the Indians unmercifully.

In 1711 the resentful Tuscaroras struck. They raided settlements, burning, scalping and murdering. The colonists had no army and no defenses. Thanks to the unscrupulous traders who had sold guns to the Indians, the Tuscaroras were better armed than the settlers.

Without the aid of its sister colonies to the north and south, North Carolina might have been destroyed. South Carolina and Virginia came to the rescue with men and money. Their soldiers, joining with hastily raised North Carolina militia, broke the Tuscaroras' power in two bloody battles.

By that time the colony was in frightful condition. The whole countryside had been laid waste. All trade was at a standstill, and the expense of the war had piled up an enormous debt.

While the war was going on, an important change took place. In 1712 the proprietors completely separated their two Carolina colonies. Henceforth they were officially North Carolina and South Carolina, each with its own government.

From then on North Carolina made steady progress, and it continued to have good government. In 1729 George II charged the proprietors with violating their charter and threatened to revoke it. Faced with the loss of their revenues, they sold their rights to the King, which was exactly what he wanted. Thus North

Carolina became a royal province. The change made little difference. If anything, the colony was better off under the royal governors. Most of them ruled wisely and well.

Although some new towns had been founded in the tidewater region, North Carolina was probably the most thinly settled of the colonies at that time. Then it suddenly began to grow very rapidly. When the Revolution began, the population was over 300,000. Only Massachusetts, Virginia and Pennsylvania had more people.

At first the new settlements spread from Albermarle County in the northeast all the way to Cape Fear in the south. They were chiefly along the rivers of the tidewater. Gradually, however, Scotch-Irish, Scotch Highlanders, Germans, Welsh and English poured into the piedmont and the mountainous back country.

Most of them came from Virginia and Pennsylvania, where the cost of buying or renting land was greater. But the Highlanders came directly from Scotland. England had put down a revolt there, and the King offered a pardon to all rebels who would swear allegiance to Britain and go to America. The new settlers had no trouble supporting themselves. Almost all were farmers, and tobacco was a profitable crop in the large area where it could be grown.

Unlike Virginia, which depended almost entirely

upon tobacco, North Carolina had two other important sources of revenue. All through its coastal plain
were forests of long-leaf pines. From them, naval
stores—tar, pitch and turpentine—could be obtained.
These products were in great demand in England,
especially the tar and pitch used to calk the wooden
ships in order to make them watertight.

Lumbering was the other great industry. The pines
provided boards; oaks supplied stout timbers and
staves, heads and hoops for barrels. In the swamps
grew cypresses, whose wood is almost impervious to
moisture and thus makes excellent shingles.

North Carolina's growing prosperity was different
from Virginia's. Although some tobacco planters and
producers of naval stores grew rich, most of the plantations were small. They could not provide the wealth
for as many great mansions, lavish furnishings imported from England or the luxurious life of Virginia
planters. And while North Carolina too had imported
slaves, there were far fewer of them than in Virginia.

In the remote back country the settlers had to
depend upon the land and the forests for almost everything. They raised corn, wheat, peas, beans and other
crops. Flax and hemp gave them materials for spinning
and weaving cloth. For shoes and heavier clothing they
tanned hides and used deerskins. They made their own
candles and soap. The forests supplied abundant

timber for their needs.

The settlers did manage to export a good many of their products to England and the West Indies. In spite of their lack of good harbors, they developed some seaports. The best was Brunswick on the Cape Fear River, and later Wilmington, a few miles farther up.

During the earlier colonial wars, North Carolina suffered little, but it did have a serious problem at that time with pirates. After the English government cleared out a nest of raiders with a stronghold in the Bahama Islands, some of them moved to the North Carolina coast. In spite of its shoals and shallow water, it proved an excellent base of operations.

The most notorious of these pirates was Edward Teach. He was better known as Blackbeard because his whole face was covered with a thick, unkempt black beard which gave him a frightful appearance.

The evidence is strong that Robert Eden, the un-principled governor of North Carolina, made a deal with Blackbeard in return for a share of his profits. The pirate and his men calmly moved into Bath, near the mouth of the Pamlico River. There they estab-lished their base. When they returned from a voyage, they sold their booty to traders there. No one, least of all Governor Eden, molested them.

Decent citizens of Bath, who were terrified by the

pirates' roistering, complained in vain. So did the governors of Virginia and South Carolina, whose ships were also being seized and plundered. At last Governor Alexander Spotswood of Virginia took action. He fitted out two armed sloops and sent them after the pirates, who were cruising off the coast. The searchers sighted their quarry in Ocracoke Inlet, not far from Cape Hatteras, and gave chase.

Blackbeard's ship, armed with nine cannon, ran aground. One of the Virginia vessels also grounded, but the other, in charge of a British naval officer, Lieutenant Robert Maynard, closed in.

Like cornered rats, Blackbeard and his men stormed aboard the Virginia sloop. On deck there was a fierce hand-to-hand fight. Blackbeard's ferocious appearance did not daunt the fearless Maynard. He engaged the pirate leader in a duel with swords, killed him and struck off his head.

The expedition returned to Virginia in triumph, with Blackbeard's head suspended from the end of the bowsprit. Fourteen of the pirates were hanged. That put an end to piracy along the coast.

As for the Colonial wars, North Carolina's only danger in Queen Anne's War came from the sea, when French warships raided settlements along the coast. In King George's War, when Spain was also an enemy, Spanish privateers attacked and plundered the seaports of Brunswick and Beaufort. Although the colony was never threatened on land, it did send soldiers to the frontiers of other colonies in both King George's and the French and Indian War.

More serious was the colonists' revolt against a royal governor named William Tryon. Governor Tryon had come from England in 1765 to rule North Carolina. In many ways he was an excellent governor, but he was headstrong and he could be cruel. One of his first acts was to build a magnificent palace. It served not only as the provincial capitol at New Bern but also as his own residence. And it cost so much money that taxes had to be raised.

This enraged the poorer settlers of the back country. There was much corruption in that region. Some of the taxes collected by the sheriffs went into their own pockets. Court officers demanded outrageous fees for legal documents they issued. When the settlers could not pay their taxes, the sheriffs seized and sold their houses and other possessions.

Tryon knew of the corruption and disapproved of it, but he did nothing. At last the backwoodsmen took matters into their own hands. They were rough, pugnacious men, and oppression had made them lawless. They organized an armed band known as the Regulators.

The Regulators swore to assist each other in resisting

the officials' tyranny. In 1770 a group of them rushed the courthouse in the settlement of Hillsborough. They beat court officers savagely, including one of the most notorious grafters, and forced the judge to flee for his life.

When such riots continued, Tryon called out the militia. Few responded, since most of the people were in sympathy with the Regulators. Tryon finally managed to assemble about 1,100 men and marched for the back country. There he met two thousand armed Regulators at Great Alamance Creek. In a furious battle the rebels were routed, and their leader was executed on the battlefield.

Tryon's cruel streak then showed itself. Not content with having broken the Regulators' power, he marched through the countryside, burning their homes and laying waste their farms. Twelve Regulators were tried, found guilty of treason, and six were hanged.

For a long time North Carolina, the sickly child of the American colonies, straggled along without much government or the strong guiding hand of any one man. But eventually, almost in spite of itself, the colony succeeded. Its fine natural resources played a large part in its ultimate success. So did the strong will and determination of its settlers, who struggled against great difficulties all through colonial times.

# chapter 12

# Land of Rice and Indigo

When the proprietors of Carolina, dissatisfied with their colony in the northern part of their grant, decided to try again in the south, theirs was not the first settlement in that region. Nearly 150 years earlier, the Spaniards in Florida had explored the coast of what is now South Carolina. They established a few trading posts, but none of them lasted. Nevertheless, Spain claimed this territory.

Forty years later, persecuted Huguenots from France made a settlement on the coast. They called it Port Royal. But they were afflicted with famine, homesickness, quarreling and Spanish harassment, and they abandoned it.

In 1669 the English proprietors of Carolina fitted out three ships for the southern region. They gave much more thought to planning this second colony.

Provisions, tools and implements in abundance were loaded aboard the vessels. Yet actually their concern was less for the colonists' welfare than their own. Their main idea was to make money from their venture.

Two of the vessels were wrecked in the West Indies during the voyage. The largest one, the *Carolina,* arrived on the Carolina coast in March, 1670. She went first to the abandoned settlement of Port Royal. But one of the leaders warned that it was too much exposed to attack from the Spaniards. The rest of the group heeded his counsel, and the *Carolina* sailed on to the mouth of the Ashley River.

There, on the river's western bank, the colonists established their settlement. They named it Charles Town in honor of the King. There were about 140 people, almost all English, plus others who had joined en route. Among the group were indentured servants, freemen, and 16 women.

Not long afterward a lone man arrived at Charles Town. His name was Henry Woodward, and his coming was probably the luckiest thing that could have happened to the little town. More than any other original settler of South Carolina, he was responsible for its survival and early prosperity.

Woodward had lived in Barbados in the West Indies. While planning this second colony, the Carolina proprietors had wisely sent him to southern Carolina to look over the country. He went to Port Royal and remained among the Indians there for some time while he explored the surrounding territory.

In Florida, the Spaniards heard that Woodward was in the region. A raiding party set out, seized the Englishman and bore him off to the Spanish stronghold of St. Augustine. But he managed to escape and make his way north to the new English settlement.

Woodward then set out to win the friendship of the Indians in the neighborhood of Charles Town. He treated them with kindness and understanding and won their good will for the settlement. Then he journeyed far into the interior and made a treaty of peace with the ferocious Westos. Thus the broad valley of the Savannah River, the present boundary between South Carolina and Georgia, was opened to trade.

Woodward had done a service of the greatest importance to the colony. Ships from England came to Charles Town loaded with hoes, axes, guns, cloth, brass rings and beads. For these articles the Indians eagerly exchanged their valuable furs and deerskins. For many years this was South Carolina's chief source of income.

More settlers soon came. In February, 1671, two ships arrived with 112 from Barbados. In fact, so many Barbadians settled in Charles Town during the next few years that in some ways it resembled a West

Indian town.

The proprietors had provided plenty of food to see the colony through the first year, and the settlers expected that this source of supply would continue. Since they were busy trading with the Indians and also with lumbering, they did not worry too much about planting food crops. They did clear thirty acres of land, however, put up houses and surround their town with a stout palisade.

Before very long, however, the colonists decided the site they had selected was too marshy and therefore unhealthful. Also, the river was not deep enough there for large ships. Charles Town was moved to a neck of land between the Ashley and Etiwa rivers, two miles away. Here there was an excellent harbor.

All seemed well, but before long the proprietors in England began to complain. They demanded that a large share of the Indian trade be set aside for them, as well as some of the best land. They also complained that the quitrents due them were not being paid.

The proprietors then stopped sending food and supplies. Soon the settlement was menaced by starvation, and the settlers realized their mistake in not planting more food crops.

Joseph West, the governor of the colony, was trusted by both the proprietors and the people. He suggested that the colonists agree not to trade more than 100

miles from Charles Town. They were to leave the country beyond to the proprietors.

This satisfied both sides, and the shipping of food and supplies from England was resumed. Again Henry Woodward did the colony a great service. He managed the Indian trade in the back country for the proprietors, seeing to it that they received the profits and that other traders kept out.

For some time everything went smoothly. New settlers came from Barbados. And in less than a month 500 people who were fleeing persecution in England arrived at the colony. Also from England came a large number of Huguenot exiles who had been unable to make a living there. In addition the proprietors sent Scots, who settled near Port Royal. And even some Puritans from frigid New England came to this warmer land. In two years the colony's population doubled from about 1,100 to 2,200.

Indian trade was still the most important occupation. Each spring, Charles Town was jammed with pack horses loaded with furs. They clopped into town with their bells jangling. Long files of Indians with bundles of skins on their backs padded through the narrow streets in their moccasins to the wharves where ships lay ready to load the precious cargo.

Two other profitable sources of revenue soon developed. A ship from Madagascar in the Indian Ocean arrived at Charles Town with rice from that far-off island. Soon many farmers were raising rice in the rich bottom lands of the coastal lowlands. It became South Carolina's most important crop, bringing immense wealth to the colony.

The second development was the growing of indigo, the plant used in making a beautiful blue dye. For this, South Carolina owed much to a young girl who discovered how to raise it profitably.

Elizabeth Lucas was the daughter of an English army officer who had bought large tracts of land in South Carolina. When war between England and Spain began in 1739, he was appointed military governor of Antigua in the West Indies. Eliza, as she was called, was then 17. She was a capable girl, intensely interested in agriculture, and her father left her in charge of his Carolina plantations.

From Antigua he sent her some indigo seed. People in the South Carolina colony had already tried to raise indigo, but it hadn't done well. In 1741, Eliza began to experiment with it. Three years later she had her first crop of good indigo. In no time it became second only to rice among South Carolina's chief crops.

The prosperity which came from rice and indigo also brought trouble. Raising these crops required hands who could work in the fields under the blazing summer sun. Negroes were best suited to it, and great numbers of slaves were brought in. More than any other colony, South Carolina was ridden with slavery.

And Negroes were not the only people enslaved. Traders in the back country found it profitable to round up Indians and sell them into slavery. Some were bought by South Carolina planters, but more were shipped to the West Indies and sold there.

These unscrupulous traders also abused and cheated the Indians. In the early years, Henry Woodward had kept the natives peaceful. Even after his death, South Carolina remained safe for a time because there were so many small tribes who were not united against abuse by the whites.

At last, however, in 1715, the Creek, Apalachee, Yamassee and other tribes, egged on by the Spaniards in Florida and the French in Louisiana, united and struck. Because the Carolina authorities had done nothing to curb the traders' dishonesty and cruelty, South Carolina came close to being completely destroyed.

Seven thousand warriors raided the countryside. Many settlers were massacred or tortured to death. The roads were choked with people who abandoned their villages and fled to Charles Town, the only safe refuge. Soon colonial troops marched against the Indians, who were finally beaten. Many were captured or sold into slavery, while others moved to Florida. For a time the Indian menace was ended.

Shortly afterward, South Carolina had an uprising among its own people. For years the proprietors in England had run the colony to suit themselves, and the settlers had little to say about their government. There was an elected Assembly, but the real power lay with the governor and his Council, appointed by the proprietors.

In 1718 a dispute arose in the Assembly over the quitrents the people had to pay the proprietors. It was the same complaint settlers of other colonies had had. The colonists felt they should own the land themselves.

The governor at the time—Robert Johnson—was well liked, and he tried to look after the interests of the people. He wanted to settle their grievance. The proprietors, however, ordered him to dismiss the Assembly and have a new one elected which would do their bidding.

The new Assembly turned out to be even more rebellious. Its members angrily voted to declare that the proprietors' rule was at an end. Then they sent an agent to London to tell the King.

Their bold action succeeded. George I made South Carolina a royal province, and the greedy proprietors lost their colony. From then almost until the Revolution, most of the governors were good men, and on the whole things went well.

Except for trouble with the Indians, South Carolina was concerned very little with the colonial wars. During King George's War, however, the French stirred the powerful Cherokees to raid frontier settlements. At that time South Carolina had one of its best governors, James Glen. When the Cherokees went on the warpath, he stopped all trade with them and persuaded Virginia and Georgia to do the same. Since English implements, cloth, glittering beads and other baubles were dear to the Indians' hearts, they changed their minds and made peace.

Again, during the French and Indian War, the French incited the Cherokees to make war, and many white settlements were raided. South Carolina militia and British Regulars marched into the Cherokee country, laid waste Indian villages, killed hundreds of warriors and took others prisoner. Then, in a great battle, the remaining Cherokees were beaten; their power was broken forever.

During this period of the eighteenth century, settlement of the colony increased rapidly. Towns were established in the coastal plain and the piedmont by Swiss, Germans, Huguenots, Scotch-Irish, Welsh and English settlers. By 1761 people from Pennsylvania and Virginia were pouring into the back country and the mountains.

Rice and indigo were South Carolina's chief prod-

ucts, but many of the new settlers raised other crops—
flax, hemp, wheat, corn—and bred livestock. The Huguenots planted mulberry trees and the worms that fed
on them produced silk. South Carolina also had a large
belt of long-leaf pines which furnished naval stores.

Of all the settlements, Charles Town (its name was
changed to Charleston about the time of the Revolution) was by far the most important. The rice and
indigo plantations of the surrounding countryside
made vast fortunes for their owners. Many built
splendid mansions in Charles Town, where they lived
in summer to escape the stifling heat and malaria of
the low marshlands.

Merchants, too, who handled South Carolina's export and import trade, grew rich and had their fine
houses. Some owned their own fleets of ships, though
few vessels were built in the colony. Charles Town
was a bustling seaport.

It also became a center of culture and luxury. Some
of its great houses, built in the beautiful Georgian
style, can still be seen today. Their furnishings were
the finest England could supply. Merchants and
planters and their families dressed in silk and satin.
They lived in splendor like that of rich English noble-
men, perhaps even greater than that of the wealthy
Virginia tobacco planters. All this wealth had been
brought to South Carolina by rice and indigo—and

the cheap labor of wretched slaves.

Far different were conditions in the back country. The settlements there, remote from the capital at Charles Town, were neglected. The people were poor and shamefully overtaxed. There were no courts to settle their grievances, and in place of government there was only disorder.

Desperation finally forced the back-country people into action. The Regulators who caused such trouble and strife in North Carolina were first organized in South Carolina. There were riots and bloodshed, but it was not until 1761 that the back country was finally given courts and orderly government.

South Carolina's settlement and growth were, in their own way, like those of Virginia. The Jamestown colonists had John Smith to guide them through difficult times; South Carolina had Henry Woodward. Virginia had tobacco to bring it easy prosperity; South Carolina had rice and indigo to provide a way of life as luxurious as Virginia's. By the middle years of the eighteenth century, South Carolina did not have to envy any of its sister colonies in America.

# chapter 13

# The Last of the Colonies

It has been said that Georgia was settled by convicts. This is not so. True, a good many of the original settlers came out of English prisons, but they were unfortunate people who had been unable to pay their debts. Not one was a real criminal.

In London, the Fleet, the Marshalsea and other terrible debtors' prisons were crowded with these wretched people. Those who were poor were almost certainly doomed to spend the rest of their lives there, ill-treated and living in squalor. Since they could not work, they had little chance of getting money to pay what they owed.

James Oglethorpe was the savior of these poor debtors. Although well off, he was not a rich man, but he was a philanthropist by nature. In fact, it seemed as if he had a heart as big as the vast wilderness of America.

As a young man, Oglethorpe served in the British army. Then he was elected to Parliament. As a member of a committee appointed to investigate conditions in the prisons, he had his first chance to see the poor debtors' misery. What he saw gave him an excellent idea.

England wanted colonists for America. Oglethorpe thought that if debtors could be released to go there it would be not only to the government's but to the settlers' and their creditors' advantage. By making a way for themselves in the New World, the debtors might be able to pay what they owed.

Oglethorpe had influential friends. They banded together, and in 1732 obtained a charter for land "on the southwest of Carolina," to be called Georgia in honor of King George II. The colony was to be administered by 20 of the group, known as the trustees. Since Oglethorpe was a military man and the colony would be menaced by the Spaniards, he was to go along as its head.

Far from accepting criminals, the trustees took the greatest care in investigating the character of those who applied. They also insisted that all debtors must get their creditors' permission to go. Not all the colonists were from the prisons. Other unfortunate people of London were also allowed to apply.

A committee of over a hundred clergymen set about to obtain money and gifts of supplies and equipment for the expedition. In the fall of 1732 all was ready, and more than a hundred people had been accepted. The ship *Anne* of 200 tons sailed with them and arrived at Charles Town in January, 1733.

The South Carolinians were delighted to have the neighbor colony. It would be a bulwark between them and the Spaniards in Florida, who were always threatening. South Carolina gave the newcomers horses, cattle, sheep, hogs, rice and £2,000.

From Charles Town, Oglethorpe took his flock to a bluff about 18 miles above the mouth of the Savannah River. They landed February 12, 1733, and set up four large tents they had brought. Oglethorpe then laid out the town of Savannah with broad streets which had squares at intervals for market places. Savannah was to accommodate 24 families. Later, the trustees planned other settlements spreading out into the countryside.

Oglethorpe did not forget the Indians' rights. He held a parley with the chiefs of the principal Creek tribes, who granted the land to the whites and signed a treaty of peace and friendship.

Thus the youngest and last of the American colonies began. More than a century and a quarter had passed since the first permanent settlement had been established in Virginia.

Like William Penn and Roger Williams, the trustees thought of their colony as a holy experiment. Yet it was to be different from Pennsylvania and Rhode Island. Only Protestants were to be allowed to settle in Georgia.

Jews came too, however. They managed it cleverly. In London, three of them, desperate over their people's troubles there, got permission to solicit money for the colony. Instead of turning it over to the trustees, they used it to send 40 of their number to Georgia.

Once they arrived, Oglethorpe saw there was little he could do about it. To expel them would be difficult. Besides, his compassionate heart would not let him send them back to misery in England. He gave them land and made them welcome.

Settlements soon began to increase. The trustees sent more poor debtors and unfortunates. They also recruited some Scotch Highlanders because they were good fighters. They were settled on the Altamaha River, close to Florida and the dreaded Spaniards.

Persecuted Protestants from other parts of Europe also came—Lutherans and Moravians from Austria, as well as Germans and Swiss. In 1734 Oglethorpe went to England. While he was there a benevolent Parliament granted £26,000 to foster immigration to

Georgia. The trustees soon had 1,100 applications. When Oglethorpe returned in 1736 he brought more English settlers and more supplies and equipment.

When danger loomed from the Spaniards to the south, Oglethorpe fortified some of the islands just off the coast. Then he invited the Spanish leaders to come and see them. They seemed impressed and signed a peace treaty, but they soon broke it. During England's war with Spain, which began in 1739, a Spanish force advanced from St. Augustine against the Georgia forts.

For all his humanity and good works, Oglethorpe was a formidable military commander. When a Spanish detachment advanced to attack Fort Frederica, the principal Georgia border stronghold, he gave it a terrible beating and killed or captured a good part of the men. With that, the main Spanish army turned tail and slunk back to Florida.

Although the Spanish invasion threat was ended, the colony was not prospering. The first flood of immigration had slackened. Those who had already come found it difficult to exist.

In spite of their zeal to see that Georgia was a model colony, the trustees had made two bad mistakes. First, they tried to tell the colonists how they must live, work and behave themselves. They knew almost nothing about Georgia or its possibilities, yet they decided that the chief occupation was to be raising silk. Every landholder had to plant at least a hundred mulberry trees for feeding silkworms.

The trustees were so anxious to prevent land speculation that they limited the amount each settler was to have. Most of them were allowed from ten to fifty acres. However, in order to attract people of some means, they granted 500 acres to anyone who paid his own passage and brought ten servants.

Again, in order to prevent settlers from selling their land to speculators, the trustees did not allow the colonists to own it. To overcome this disadvantage, no quitrents were to be charged for ten years.

Slavery was forbidden in Georgia. Nor were settlers allowed to bring strong liquor into the colony.

The settlers rebelled against raising silk. The climate was not ideal for it and, although some silk was produced, the amount grew steadily less. Besides, Georgia offered far better possibilities for prosperity.

Its large areas of pine forests could produce naval stores. Rice would grow well in the colony's swampy lowlands. The settlers turned jealous eyes upon South Carolina, where rice was making such fortunes for planters.

The second mistake of the trustees was not to establish a proper government for Georgia. The colony's charter provided for a governor to be named by the trustees, but they never appointed one. They ruled Georgia by the rules and regulations they set up themselves.

Oglethorpe was considered the head of the colony, but he was able to supervise only Savannah and the nearby settlements. Some of the more distant towns set up their own governments; others had none at all.

The people rebelled against all the trustees' rules and regulations. They felt it was their own business whether they drank or not. Soon taverns and grog shops sprang up in defiance of a ban against them.

The colonists were especially bitter at the prohibition against keeping slaves, who were so necessary for working the rice fields. They began to bring them into Georgia secretly.

At last the people sent an agent to England to submit their grievances to Parliament. But its members made the man fall on his knees while he was reprimanded for his audacity in complaining.

Oglethorpe himself was not in sympathy with the trustees' overbearing rule. He felt they had not supported him in improving conditions in Georgia. In 1743 he sailed for England, never to return.

But the trustees knew a reckoning was coming. Their charter was for a period of just 21 years. They feared the King would lend a sympathetic ear to the colonists and take over the colony at that time. Gradually, they relaxed their regulations.

First they did away with the rule against rum. In 1749 they allowed limited slavery in Georgia. The next year they removed the rule against buying and selling land. And in 1751 they ordered an Assembly chosen by the people to meet in Savannah.

It was a mockery of a legislature, however. The representatives were not allowed to make laws. They could only discuss ways of improving Georgia's sad condition.

The trustees desperately needed money to keep the colony going. Parliament refused to grant it. So did the King, unless the trustees would surrender their charter. They had little choice but to agree, and in 1752 Georgia became a royal province.

The great experiment had failed. Yet it had not failed in its original purpose to give downtrodden people a chance to make a new and better life for themselves in Georgia. And although Ogelthorpe's cherished plan had not worked out fully, he lived to see the colony prosper and become a free state of the United States.

As a royal province, Georgia had a governor, lieutenant governor and Council appointed by the King. They formed the upper house of the Assembly. The lower one, elected by the people, was the Commons House. The Assembly could pass laws, though the

King could disapprove them. Courts were set up in the colony.

Georgia now made steady progress. Even the French and Indian War did little to hamper it. Although the colony was almost surrounded by Indian tribes, the Indians did not attack. French privateers raided some coastal settlements, but did little damage. And Georgia was too small and weak to send troops to the war areas when England asked the colony for aid.

As soon as the war ended, new settlers flooded in. When the King took over the colony, it had only about 2,000 people. When the Revolution began there were 33,000.

Of these, 15,000 were slaves. They were brought in when the settlers at last won the right to plant rice and indigo. Among these plantations were those of 350 Puritans who had left Massachusetts for South Carolina and then migrated to Georgia. They brought 1,500 slaves with them.

Georgia was raising rice, indigo, wheat, corn and livestock. The forests produced naval stores, lumber, shingles and staves. The town of Augusta was the largest fur-trading center in the southern colonies, and Savannah had become an important seaport.

Georgia is the colony that failed yet succeeded. Its founders did a great service to poor and unfortunate people. Georgia stands with Rhode Island, Maryland

and Pennsylvania as a colony begun as a haven for the oppressed. Its founders failed, but its settlers turned the failure into victory by making this youngest American colony survive and go on to prosperity.

# chapter 14

# The Coming of
the Revolution

In their early years the American colonies were like
thirteen separate small nations. Each had its own problems, and there was little to make them act together
for the good of all.

But during the middle years of the eighteenth century, British oppression gradually unified them. Thus
it is well to look at all thirteen together as the struggle
against tyranny began.

Massachusetts led the way. Its resistance actually
began late in the seventeenth century with the trouble over the Navigation Acts and the revolt against
Andros. In the years that followed, Massachusetts
merchants continued to ignore the Navigation Acts, as
well as the Sugar Act, which imposed a customs duty
on sugar and molasses brought from the West Indies.

Britain was determined, perhaps rightfully, to get

some sort of revenue from the American colonies. On the other hand, the Americans felt that this was their land. They had hewn their homes out of the wilderness and overcome hardships without much help from the government in London. What they resented most was that some of their rights as free Englishmen were being taken away, especially by taxes imposed without their consent.

In Massachusetts, as well as other colonies, goods were being smuggled ashore successfully in spite of the king's customs officers, who tried to stop this contraband trade. In England, Parliament then passed a law by which customs officers could be armed with documents called writs of assistance. This enabled them to search wherever they pleased for contraband—in a merchant's warehouse, even in a private house. A suit over the law was brought to court.

James Otis, a giant of a man, bull-necked and broad-shouldered, stormed up and down the courtroom, lecturing judges and jury in a voice like a thunderclap. He charged that the writs of assistance violated Magna Carta, the great English document upon which many of our own freedoms as well as those of Englishmen are based. He did not win the suit, but he sounded a trumpet call which echoed all through the American colonies.

Then the English Parliament passed the Stamp Act.

It placed a tax on the American colonies without their consent. Stamps had to be purchased and put on almost everything that was printed—deeds, wills, ships' clearance papers, newspapers, even college diplomas and marriage certificates.

Massachusetts, the most belligerent of the colonies, showed its independence when a howling Boston mob of two thousand stormed the house of Andrew Oliver. Oliver had been appointed stamp master to distribute the stamps. They demolished the furniture, then rushed to a small building put up as the stamp office and tore it down.

Next they burst into the elegant mansion of Thomas Hutchinson, the lieutenant governor. They smashed everything in it—furniture, paintings, clocks, fine china, even the paneled walls. Then they ripped off the roof, leaving it a ruined shell.

The rebellious spirit also erupted in Virginia. It happened in Williamsburg, which had replaced Jamestown as the capital of the colony. Originally known as the Middle Plantation, it had been renamed in honor of King William III.

At one end of Williamsburg's broad, mile-long main street stood the new capitol building. At the other end was Virginia's first college, the second in America—William and Mary. Between them were the governor's magnificent palace, shops and massive, splendid houses, many built by planters who were burgesses and lived in them while the Assembly was in session.

Today Williamsburg may be seen, restored in all its glory, as it looked in 1765 when Patrick Henry, a red-haired, six-foot beanpole, stood before the Assembly to protest the Stamp Act. His blue eyes blazed as he thundered the celebrated words: "Tarquin and Caesar each had his Brutus, Charles the First his Cromwell, and George the Third——"

Some of his hearers were not ready for a tirade against the King. As Henry paused, the speaker of the Assembly cried, "Treason!" and others echoed him.

Then Henry finished: "——may profit by their example!" It has been said that he added, "If *this* be treason, make the most of it!"

There were enough devoted patriots in the Assembly to pass some of Henry's resolutions against the Stamp Act.

The rest of the colonies also protested. In some, mobs forced the stamp masters to resign; in others, the law was simply ignored. Lawyers were much affected, since all legal documents had to have stamps affixed. In New Jersey they agreed to buy none, even if they had to give up their livelihood by refusing to do any legal business.

The tyrannical Governor Tryon of North Carolina

called out the militia to enforce the Stamp Act. The soldiers were reluctant, but Tryon attempted to win them to his side with a barbecued ox and plenty of beer. They dumped the ox into the river and knocked in the heads of the beer barrels.

In New York, a mob stoned British soldiers stationed there. At the same time, New York patriots took a much more important action. Representatives from all thirteen colonies were invited to meet in New York City to protest the Stamp Act.

The colonies were not yet well united, but nine of them did send delegates to what became known as the Stamp Act Congress. It was the first time that even as many as nine colonies had united to take action. A petition was sent to the King demanding repeal of the Stamp Act. It declared that only the colonies' assemblies could impose taxes upon the people.

The British government saw its mistake and repealed the Stamp Act. A little later, however, Parliament passed the Townshend Acts, which placed customs duties on glass, lead, paint, paper and tea. A number of the colonies retaliated with non-importation agreements by which merchants agreed not to trade with England. Parliament then repealed the Townshend Acts too.

The trouble was far from over in Massachusetts, however. After the Stamp Act riots, Governor Francis

Bernard demanded that England send soldiers to Boston, and almost four thousand of them came. When the Stamp Act was repealed, the soldiers remained, stirring up hatred against themselves and King George III.

Boys taunted the redcoats, calling them "lobsters" and "bloodybacks," pelting them with stones, clamshells, rotten eggs and spoiled fruit. Men picked fights with them. Boston was split into two factions—the patriots and those they contemptuously called Tories, men who supported the royal government.

On the clear, cold winter's night of March 5, 1770, a mob gathered in front of the custom house and began to badger the British sentry there. He shouted for help and a squad of soldiers marched from the nearby guardhouse. There was a scuffle and the redcoats fired into the crowd. In the bloody snow four persons lay dead and a number were wounded, one of whom later died.

This was the Boston Massacre. It roused the people to such fury that the American Revolution might have started then and there if Thomas Hutchinson, the royal governor, had not agreed to send the British regiments out of Boston.

Meanwhile, two other patriots were stirring up the colonies' resentment against English oppression. When poor James Otis' mind failed not long after his masterful handling of the suit against the writs of assistance, an able successor took his place in Massachusetts.

Samuel Adams looked as if he had just tumbled out of a rag bag. His wig was always askew; his clothes, rumpled and stained. He failed at a number of jobs and never knew where his next shilling was coming from. But one thing he could do was to write, and he did—an endless stream of letters to the Boston newspapers. His subject was always how England was taking the rights of free men away from America. Perhaps more than any other American, Sam Adams aroused the people of Massachusetts and, later, of all the colonies.

It was he who suggested forming a Committee of Correspondence to write letters to the other colonies describing Massachusetts' wrongs and what could be done to resist oppression. The others took it up, and these committees fanned the flames of resistance and aided in uniting all the colonies.

Not far behind Sam Adams in his influence upon the people was John Dickinson of Delaware. Born on a farm, he studied law in Philadelphia and then in London. In 1760 he was elected to the Delaware Assembly and became its speaker.

From the very first, Dickinson was so devoted to the cause of America's rights that his mother became worried lest he be charged with treason. "Johnny," she said, "you will be hanged and your estate will be forfeited. You will leave your excellent wife a widow and your children orphans, beggars and infamous."

He paid no heed. In 1767 the first of his 12 articles was published. These articles became famous as the "Farmer's Letters." In them he argued for the rights of free men, especially that taxes could not be imposed upon them without their consent. The letters were read throughout the colonies.

If Dickinson had foreseen the influence the Farmer's Letters would have in goading America toward revolution, he surely would never have written them. Although he was against oppression with all his heart, he was just as violently against independence. And in 1776, as a delegate to the Continental Congress, he refused to sign the Declaration of Independence.

After the Boston Massacre, England tried for a time to pacify the colonies. For three years she made no more attempts to tax the people without their consent or to violate their rights in other ways. But in Rhode Island, resistance against another form of oppression burst forth in 1772.

Rhode Island seafaring men were bothered very little at first by the British laws restricting the colonies' sea trade. They smuggled cargoes in and out of Narragansett Bay so cleverly that the King's revenue officers at Newport and Providence were at their wits' end trying to stop them.

At last England sent armed vessels to the bay. The wily shipmasters fought back by using their faster, lighter-draft ships as decoys. One of them would let a ponderous English watchdog chase her into shallow water until the man-of-war could go no farther. Then the decoy would escape. Meanwhile, other Rhode Island merchantmen would sail merrily in and out of the bay.

Nevertheless, many of the colony's ships were stopped. The English ships not only searched the Rhode Island vessels for contraband, but often took off sailors and impressed them against their will into the naval service. The warships were always short-handed, since sailors in the British navy were treated like dogs.

A bold Rhode Island shipmaster, Captain Benjamin Lindsey, decided this violation of free men's rights must end. With his ship, the *Hannah,* he sailed out of Newport and decoyed the British armed sloop *Gaspée* into shallow water, where she ran hard aground.

Ashore in Newport, patriot leaders were watching gleefully. When the *Gaspée* struck, drummers went through the streets beating a call for volunteers. That night eight longboats full of men armed with muskets rowed with muffled oars toward the stranded warship.

Sixty yards from her, they heard a challenge: "Who goes there?" It was Lieutenant William Dudingston, commanding the *Gaspée*.

Captain Abraham Whipple, the patriots' leader, replied, "I am come for the commander of this vessel, and have him I will, dead or alive! Men, spring to your oars!"

The Rhode Islanders fired a volley. Lieutenant Dudingston had come on deck without his jacket, and in his white shirt he was an excellent target, even in the darkness. He fell wounded to the deck.

The Rhode Islanders swarmed aboard the *Gaspée*, driving her crew below decks, and she surrendered. Then she was set afire.

Her cannon had been loaded. As the flames roared and crackled they heated the big guns' barrels and the powder charges exploded, one after another, with mighty blasts. They were no louder, however, than the roars that went up from an immense crowd gathered along the shore.

Then, in 1773, George III and his Parliament made another mistake. Like most Englishmen, the people of Massachusetts dearly loved their tea, but when it was taxed under the Townshend Acts they stopped drinking it. Parliament then enacted a law reducing the price of tea. Although a small customs duty was concealed in the price, tea in America would be cheaper than before. The people saw it as a trick to make them pay a tax imposed without their consent.

In December of 1773 three ships loaded with tea arrived in Boston. On the evening of the sixteenth, a group of patriots disguised as Indians rushed to Griffin's Wharf. There the "Mohawks" went quietly to work. Aboard the vessels there was scarcely a sound except the skreak of chests being ripped open, the creak of windlasses and a soft swishing as the cargoes were dumped into the harbor in the biggest and most famous Tea Party in history.

Other colonies had their tea parties. In New York, when a tea ship arrived, a mob dumped 18 chests of it overboard. At Charles Town and Georgetown in South Carolina, two tea shipments met the same fate, while other cargoes were sent back to England.

Except for Massachusetts' tea party, the one held by Maryland patriots was the most exciting. When the brig *Peggy Stewart* reached Annapolis her owner, Anthony Stewart, paid the tax and got ready to land the tea she carried.

A furious mob gathered, howling threats against Stewart. He was so frightened that he not only destroyed the tea but the *Peggy Stewart* as well.

Punishment came swiftly to Massachusetts. Thousands of British soldiers swarmed into Boston. The town was put under the iron rule of a military governor. The port was closed, and but for the aid which flooded into Boston by land from neighboring towns and other colonies, the people might have starved.

Among those who came to the rescue, North Carolina sent a whole shipload of provisions. South Carolina gave money and a thousand barrels of rice. Georgia too sent rice. But nothing touched the hearts of the people of Boston quite as much as what happened one day in August, 1774.

A vast crowd gathered and lined the streets as the word went from mouth to mouth: "It's Old Put! Old Put is here!"

Israel Putnam, of the little wilderness hamlet of Pomfret in northeastern Connecticut, was already famous all through New England. Everyone had heard the story of how this fearless man had crawled alone into a narrow, dark cave to slay the gigantic wolf which had been terrorizing the countryside, devouring sheep and pigs. Everyone knew of his heroism and hairbreadth escapes from death as a scout in the French and Indian War.

Now, having learned of Boston's distress, gray-haired Israel Putnam, dressed in a settler's rough clothing, came striding into Boston. Before him he drove a flock of frightened, bleating sheep to feed the hungry people.

War was very near now. Soon Paul Revere would make his famous ride to warn Massachusetts patriots the redcoats were coming.

It was not the first swift dash on horseback made by Revere. He acted as courier for the Boston patriots, even riding as far as Philadelphia with dispatches for the Continental Congress meeting there.

On December 13, 1774, Paul Revere clattered into Durham, New Hampshire, on a steaming horse. He bore a secret message for a New Hampshire patriot, John Sullivan.

The patriot leaders in Boston knew war was coming. They desperately needed guns and ammunition to equip an army. There was a British fort on an island in Portsmouth harbor, well stocked with military supplies. The Boston patriots had learned the British were about to send reinforcements there lest it be seized.

The message asked Sullivan to collect a force and take the fort. He acted swiftly. That very night he led a handful of young men to the island. The British captain in command had only a few soldiers, and he surrendered. Next day, 97 kegs of powder and a hundred muskets and pistols were on their way to Massachusetts.

When George III learned of it, he was so enraged that he demanded the seizure of all rebel military supplies. When a British force marched from Boston to take patriots' stores at Concord, the colonies' war for independence began.

One more thrilling act of defiance was yet to come before those farmer patriots fired "the shot heard round the world." Virginia's Patrick Henry spoke before the Second Revolutionary Convention of Virginia at Richmond. Virginia was considering whether to join the war which was now inevitable.

Henry said: "I know not what course others may take, but as for me, give me liberty or give me death!"

At least one other stirring drama took place before liberty was declared by the American colonies. Paul Revere was not the only patriot to ride on a mission of independence. The one made by Caesar Rodney of Delaware is not as famous, but its importance was great indeed. He was a man who worked for liberty under the very shadow of death.

Like John Dickinson, Rodney lived on a farm. He had already begun to work for freedom against oppression when, in 1768, an incurable growth appeared on his nose. Little was known of treating cancer in those days. Caesar Rodney was doomed to die a slow and painful death. But he went right on striving for the cause of liberty. He was one of Delaware's three delegates to the Continental Congress when the Declaration of Independence was being debated. The two others were George Read, who was against independence, and Thomas McKean, who favored it.

While Rodney was absent, the debate on the Declaration ended. A vote was to be taken the next day. Thomas McKean knew that without Rodney, Delaware's vote would be a tie. Thus the colony would not be included in the new nation. He sent a courier galloping for Delaware.

When the messenger arrived, Rodney was very sick, his face pale with suffering. But without a moment's delay he mounted, spurred his horse to a headlong pace and was off.

It was 80 miles to Philadelphia. Through a rainswept night, Caesar Rodney coursed on. In the morning this Paul Revere from Delaware reined up his tired horse at the Pennsylvania Statehouse, which stands today as Independence Hall.

He was just in time for the vote. As it turned out, Delaware's vote was unanimous for independence, for Read decided to go along also. But had it not been for the devoted Caesar Rodney it is possible that there might have been only twelve states in the new nation which was dedicated forever to liberty and the rights of free men.

This was the end of the long road to independence which really began with the colonization of America. The early settlers and those who followed them came in search of a land where they could live as free men. For more than a century and a half they struggled toward that goal and at last they achieved it when the colonies declared themselves free and independent and fought hard to ensure that freedom.

# BIBLIOGRAPHY

Adams, Charles Francis. *Three Episodes of Massachusetts History*. Boston: Houghton, Mifflin & Co., 1892.

Andrews, Charles M. *The Colonial Period of American History*. New Haven: Yale University Press, 1934.

Andrews, Matthew Page. *History of Maryland*. Garden City: Doubleday, Doran & Co., 1929.

—— *The Founding of Maryland*. Baltimore: Williams & Wilkins Co., 1933.

Barbour, Philip L. *The Three Worlds of Captain John Smith*. Boston: Houghton Mifflin Co., 1964.

Barker, Charles A. "The Revolutionary Impulse in Maryland." Maryland Historical Society Magazine, Vol. 36, No. 2, June, 1941.

Bartlett, John Henry. *A Synoptic History of the Granite State*. Chicago: M. A. Donohue & Co., 1939.

Bolton, Herbert Eugene and Marshall, Thomas Maitland. *The Colonization of North America, 1492–1783*. New York: Macmillan Co., 1920.

Bowen, Catherine Drinker. *John Adams and the American Revolution*. Boston: Little, Brown & Co., 1950.

Brantly, William T. *The English in Maryland, 1632–1691*. (In *Narrative and Critical History of America*.) Boston: Houghton, Mifflin Co., 1884.

Broadhead, John Romeyn. "Memoir of the Colonization of New Netherland." New York Historical Society Collections, Series 2, Vol. 2, 1849.

Carroll, Charles. *Rhode Island—Three Centuries of Democracy*. New York: Lewis Historical Publishing Co., 1932.

Chatterton, E. Keble. *Captain John Smith*. London: John Lane, The Bodley Head, Ltd., 1927.

Church, Leslie F. *Oglethorpe: a Study of Philanthropy in England and Georgia*. London: Epworth Press, 1932.

Colbourne, H. Trevor. "John Dickinson, Historical Revolutionary." Pennsylvania Magazine of History and Biography, Vol. 83, No. 3, July 1959.

Coleman, R. V. *The First Frontier.* New York: Charles Scribner's Sons, 1948.

Coulter, E. Merton. *A Short History of Georgia.* Chapel Hill: University of North Carolina Press, 1933.

Crouse, Anna and Russel. *Peter Stuyvesant of Old New York.* New York: Random House (Landmark), 1954.

Easton, Emily. *Roger Williams, Prophet and Pioneer.* Boston: Houghton Mifflin Co., 1930.

Edmunds, Pocahontas Wright. *The Pocahontas-John Smith Story.* Richmond: Dietz Press, Inc., 1956.

Ellis, David M., Frost, James A., Syrett, Harold C. and Carman, Henry J. *A Short History of New York State.* Ithaca: Cornell University Press in cooperation with the New York State Historical Association, 1957.

Ernst, James. *Roger Williams, New England Firebrand.* New York: Macmillan Co., 1932.

Forbes, Esther. *Paul Revere and the World He Lived In.* Boston: Houghton Mifflin Co., 1942.

Forman, Henry Chandlee. *Jamestown and St. Mary's.* Baltimore: Johns Hopkins Press, 1938.

Fortenbaugh, Robert and Tarman, H. James. *Pennsylvania, the Story of a Commonwealth.* Harrisburg: The Pennsylvania Book Service, 1940.

Gipson, Lawrence Henry. "An Anomalous American Colony." Pennsylvania History, Vol. 27, No. 2, April, 1960.

Gleeson, Paul F. *Rhode Island, the Development of a Democracy.* Providence: Rhode Island State Board of Education, 1957.

Hale, Nathaniel C. *Virginia Adventurer—a Historical Biography of William Claiborne.* Richmond: Dietz Press, 1951.

Hard, Walter. *The Connecticut.* New York: Rinehart & Co., 1947.

Hart, Albert Bushnell (ed.) *Commonwealth History of Massachusetts.* New York: States History Co., 1927.

Hatch, Charles E. *Jamestown, Virginia.* Washington: Government Printing Office, 1949.

Hayward, Marshall DeLancey. *Governor William Tryon and His Administration in the Province of North Carolina.* Raleigh: Alfred Williams & Co., 1903.

Hemphill, William Edwin, Schlegel, Marvin Wilson and Engelberg, Sadie Ethel. *Cavalier Commonwealth.* New York: McGraw-Hill Book Co., 1957.

Hudson, J. Paul. *A Pictorial Study of Jamestown, Virginia.* Richmond: Garrett & Massie, Inc. (no date).

Ingle, Edward. "Captain Richard Ingle, the Maryland 'Pirate and Rebel.'" Maryland Historical Society Fund—Publication No. 19, 1884.

Johnson, Amanda. *Georgia as Colony and State.* Atlanta: Walter W. Brown Publishing Co., 1938.

Jones, Charles C. *The History of Georgia.* Boston: Houghton Mifflin Co., 1883.

Kessler, Henry H. and Rachlis, Eugene. *Peter Stuyvesant and His New York.* New York: Random House, 1959.

Konkle, Burton Alva. *The Life of Andrew Hamilton.* Philadelphia: National Publishing Co., 1941.

Lamdin, Robert Dawson. "Ship-Building on the Chesapeake." Maryland Historical Magazine, Vol. 36, No. 2, June, 1941.

Lefler, Hugh Talmadge and Newsome, Albert Ray. *North Carolina.* Chapel Hill: University of North Carolina Press.

Louhi, E. A. *The Delaware Finns.* New York: The Humanity Press, 1925.

McClintock, John N. *The History of New Hampshire.* Boston: B. B. Russell, 1889.

McCormick, Richard P. *New Jersey from Colony to State,* in New Jersey Historical Series, Vol. 1. Princeton, N. J.: D. Van Nostrand Co., 1964.

McCrady, Edward. *The History of South Carolina Under the Royal Government, 1719–1776.* New York: Macmillan Co., 1899.

McDavid, Mattie Owen. *Princess Pocahontas.* New York: Neale Publishing Co., 1907.

McSherry, James. *History of Maryland.* Baltimore: John Murphy, 1849.

May, Ralph. *Early Portsmouth History.* Boston: C. E. Goodspeed & Co., 1926.

Meade, Robert Douthat. *Patrick Henry, Patriot in the Making.* Philadelphia: J. B. Lippincott Co., 1957.

Miers, Earl Schenck. *Blood of Freedom*. Williamsburg: Colonial Williamsburg, 1958.

Miller, John C. *Origins of the American Revolution*. Boston: Little, Brown & Co., 1943.

Mills, Lewis Sprague. *The Story of Connecticut*. New York: Charles Scribner's Sons, 1932.

Morgan, Forrest (ed.). *Connecticut*. Hartford: Publishing Society of Connecticut, 1904.

Morgan, George. *Patrick Henry*. Philadelphia: J. B. Lippincott Co., 1929.

Morton, Richard L. *Colonial Virginia*. Chapel Hill: University of North Carolina Press, 1960.

Oliphant, Mary C. Simms. *The New Simms History of South Carolina*. Columbia, S. C.: The State Co., 1940.

Palfrey, John Gorham. *The History of New England*. Boston: Little, Brown & Co., 1859.

Parkman, Francis. *France and England in North America*. Boston: Little, Brown & Co., 1910.

Powell, Walter A. *A History of Delaware*. Boston: Christopher Publishing House, 1928.

Pringle, Patrick. *Jolly Roger*. London: Museum Press, Ltd., 1953.

Richman, Irving Berdine. *Rhode Island, Its Making and Its Meaning*. New York: G. P. Putnam's Sons, 1902.

Rutherfurd, Livingston. *John Peter Zenger*. New York: Dodd, Mead & Co., 1904.

Sanborn, Edwin D. *History of New Hampshire*. Manchester, N. H.: John B. Clarke, 1875.

Scharf, J. Thomas. *History of Delaware*. Philadelphia: L. J. Richards & Co., 1888.

Smith, Bradford. *Captain John Smith*. Philadelphia: J. B. Lippincott Co., 1953.

Smith, John (Ashton, John, Ed.). *The Adventures and Discoveries of Captain John Smith*.

────── *The True Travels, Adventures and Observations of Captain John Smith*. Richmond: Franklin Press, 1819.

Squires, James Duane. *The Granite State of the United States*. New York: American Historical Co., 1936.

Stevens, Sylvester K. *Pennsylvania, Birthplace of a Nation*. New York: Random House, 1964.

Stillé, Charles J. *The Life and Times of John Dickinson.* Philadelphia: J. B. Lippincott Co., 1891.

Straus, Oscar S. *Roger Williams, the Pioneer of Religious Liberty.* New York: D. Appleton-Century Co., 1936.

Usher, Roland G. *The Pilgrims and Their History.* New York: Macmillan Co., 1918.

Valentine, David T. *History of the City of New York.* New York: G. P. Putnam & Co., 1853.

Van Deusen, Albert E. *Connecticut.* New York: Random House, 1961.

Van Loon, Hendrick. *The Life and Times of Peter Stuyvesant.* New York: Henry Holt & Co., 1928.

Wade, Herbert Treadwell. *A Brief History of the Colonial Wars in America from 1607 to 1775.*

Wallace, David Duncan. *South Carolina, a Short History.* Chapel Hill: University of North Carolina Press, 1951.

Wallace, Paul A. W. *Pennsylvania, Seed of a Nation.* New York: Harper & Row, 1962.

Warner, Charles Willard Hoskins. *Road to Revolution.* Richmond: Garrett & Massie, 1961.

Washburn, Wilcombe E. *The Governor and the Rebel.* Chapel Hill: University of North Carolina Press.

Welles, Lemuel A. *The History of the Regicides in New England.* New York: The Grafton Press, 1927.

Wertenbaker, Thomas Jefferson. *Give Me Liberty.* Philadelphia: American Philosophical Society, 1958.

——— *The Shaping of Colonial Virginia.* New York: Russell & Russell, 1958.

Weslager, C. A. *Dutch Explorers, Traders and Settlers in the Delaware Valley.* Philadelphia: University of Pennsylvania Press, 1961.

Willison, George F. *The Pilgrim Reader.* Garden City: Doubleday & Co., 1953.

Wilstach, Paul. *Tidewater Maryland.* Indianapolis: Bobbs-Merrill Co., 1931.

Winsor, Justin (ed.). *The Memorial History of Boston.* Boston: James R. Osgood & Co., 1880.

# INDEX

# ABOUT THE AUTHOR

CLIFFORD LINDSEY ALDERMAN comes naturally by his interest in colonial America. "My great-great-great-great-great-great-great-great-great-grandfather and grandmother were John and Priscilla Alden, who came on the Mayflower in 1620," he says. "Two other ancestors fought in the American Revolution."

Most of the dozen books he has written are about colonial and Revolutionary America. Among them are *Samuel Adams, Son of Liberty* and *Joseph Brant, Chief of the Six Nations,* as well as historical novels for young people and for adults.

Mr. Alderman, a graduate of the United States Naval Academy at Annapolis, served as a commander in World War II. He now lives and writes in Seaford, New York.

# ABOUT THE ILLUSTRATOR

LEONARD EVERETT FISHER's work has been represented in many of the nation's top exhibitions. He made his solo debut in 1952 at the Edwin Hewitt Gallery in Manhattan.

Mr. Fisher has a Master's degree from the School of Fine Arts at Yale University. He has won many prizes, including the 1950 Pulitzer Prize in art, and has illustrated numerous books for young people, among them two other Landmark books.